The Amazing Power of the Blood of Jesus: Finding Redemption, Healing, and Victory Through Christ's Sacrifice

Zama Zincume

Published by ZZ, 2024.

While every precaution has been taken in the preparation of this book, the publisher assumes no responsibility for errors or omissions, or for damages resulting from the use of the information contained herein.

THE AMAZING POWER OF THE BLOOD OF JESUS: FINDING REDEMPTION, HEALING, AND VICTORY THROUGH CHRIST'S SACRIFICE

First edition. November 17, 2024.

Written by Zama Zincume.

Table of Contents

Preface: A Personal Journey to Understanding

I t was a rainy Tuesday evening in April when I first truly understood the power of the blood of Jesus.

I was in my car, in a hospital lot, tears streaming down my face. A revelation had overwhelmed me. It would change my life forever.

My mother had just received a diagnosis of stage 4 cancer.

As I sat, gripped by fear, an old hymn played on the radio – "There is Power in the Blood."

I'd sung it countless times before, but this time was different.

In that moment of vulnerability, the lyrics became a lifeline of hope. They were no longer just words.

Why I Had to Write This Book

I'VE STUDIED, TAUGHT, and experienced the power of Jesus's blood for thirty years. It is transformative.

But, when I shared these truths, I saw many believers missing out on a vital aspect of their faith.

I've witnessed:

- A young woman was finally finding freedom from decades of guilt and shame.
- A marriage restored after seemingly irreparable damage.
- Physical healings that defied medical explanation.
- Generational curses being broken in families.

- Lives are wholly transformed through this understanding.

These weren't isolated incidents. They showed that power is available to every believer that needs to be noticed or understood.

What Makes This Book Different

YOU MIGHT BE THINKING, "Another book about the blood of Jesus?

Haven't we covered this topic enough?"

I get it.

I've read many books on this subject. They were doctrinally sound, but they often lacked something. They should have noticed the practical, everyday application of these truths.

This book bridges that gap.

⸿

HERE'S WHAT MAKES IT unique:

- Real-life stories rather than just theories
- Practical applications instead of mere doctrines.
- Simple explanations of profound spiritual truths.
- Step-by-step guides for applying these principles.
- Personal testimonies that bring the teachings to life.

A Personal Note to You, the Reader

BEFORE YOU DIVE INTO this book, I want you to know something: I wrote every word with you in mind.

Whether you're:

- A new believer trying to understand the foundations of faith.
- A seasoned Christian seeking a more profound revelation.

- Someone struggling with past hurts or present battles.
- A leader looking to help others find freedom.
- Or simply someone hungry for more of God.

There's something here for you.

How This Book Came to Be

WRITING THIS BOOK HAS been challenging and rewarding.

I've spent many nights studying Scripture, consulting believers, and documenting real-life testimonies.

I've struggled to present these profound truths. I want them to be both accessible and transformative.

What you hold in your hands isn't just the result of academic study – though there's plenty of solid teaching here.

It's also:

- The fruit of countless prayers.
- The outcome of real-life ministry experiences.
- A collection of proven principles.
- A guidebook for practical applications
- A testimony of God's faithfulness.

What You Can Expect

AS YOU JOURNEY THROUGH these pages, you'll find:

- Stories that will touch your heart.
- Truths that will challenge your thinking.
- Prayers that will strengthen your faith.
- Principles that will change your life.
- Practical steps that will lead to victory.

Each chapter builds on the last. It creates a full grasp of a vital truth. You'll learn what the blood of Jesus did and how to activate its power in your life today.

An Invitation to Journey Together

I INVITE YOU TO APPROACH this book as a reader and a fellow traveller on this journey of discovery.

Feel free to:

- Underline passages that speak to you.
- Write your thoughts in the margins.
- Take time to pray through the principles.
- Share insights with others.
- Journal your experiences.

A Prayer for You

BEFORE WE BEGIN, I'D like to pray for you:

Heavenly Father, I pray for each person reading these words. Open their spiritual eyes to see fresh revelations about the power of Jesus's blood. Let these truths move from their heads to their hearts. May they learn about this power and experience it personally in their lives. In Jesus's name, Amen.

Let's begin this journey together. Turn the page with hope. What you will find could change your faith and your life.

With anticipation and faith,

Zama Zincume

P.S. I'd love to hear how this book impacts your life. Feel free to share your story at hello@zamazincume.com

Introduction: Discovering the Life-Changing Power of Jesus's Blood

Have you ever wondered why Christians talk so much about the blood of Jesus?

You've sung hymns about being "washed in the blood." You've heard "covered by the blood" in church. But you've wondered what it all means for your life today.

As a young believer, I sat in church and heard these phrases. They intrigued me but also confused me. My mind asked many questions: What is this Jesus' blood all about?

The concept seemed ancient and mysterious.

But my years of study, experience, and ministry have changed me. I have witnessed the power of Jesus's blood and believe it will transform yours, too.

Why This Book Now?

WITH TODAY'S TECH AND science, the power of blood may seem outdated.

But I've never seen a time when people needed more of what the blood of Jesus offers than now. It gives genuine forgiveness, deep healing, lasting freedom, and security.

Every day, I meet people who are:

- Struggling with guilt from their past.
- Fighting battles, they can't seem to win.

5

- Seeking healing for deep emotional wounds.
- Longing for real peace and security.
- Looking for something more meaningful in their spiritual lives.

If you identify with any of these situations, you're not alone. More importantly, you're exactly who this book was written for.

What You're About to Discover

THIS IS MORE THAN A theological book of complex doctrines and complicated concepts.

Instead, think of it as if you're sitting down with a friend. Your friend is excited to share the life-changing truths that have significantly impacted his life.

Throughout these pages, we'll explore:

- The incredible significance of blood in God's plan throughout history.
- The seven powerful ways the blood of Jesus works in our lives today.
- Practical ways to apply these truths for real-life victories
- Amazing testimonies of lives transformed by this understanding.
- Step-by-step guidance for experiencing more of God's power.

More Than Just Information

MY GOAL ISN'T JUST to inform you about the blood of Jesus.

You'll learn a lot!

I hope these pages awaken you to the power of Christ's sacrifice. It's already available to you.

This isn't about learning religious terminology or adopting church culture.

It's about discovering a source of power that can:

- Break chains that have held you back for years.
- Heal wounds you thought would never heal.
- Give you the confidence you never thought was possible.
- Transform your relationship with God.
- Equip you to help others find freedom.

How to Get the Most from This Book

AS YOU READ THROUGH these chapters, I encourage you to:

1. Keep an open heart. Some concepts might challenge your previous understanding but stay receptive to fresh insights.
2. Take your time with the material. Let each truth sink deep into your spirit.
3. Make it personal. The questions and prayers at each chapter's end will help you apply these truths to your situation.
4. Share your journey. Consider reading this with a friend or small group. Some of the most potent breakthroughs happen in the community.
5. Expect results. The power of Jesus's blood isn't just a historical fact – it's a present reality available to you right now.

A Personal Invitation

AS WE BEGIN THIS JOURNEY together, I want to share something: this book isn't meant to impart knowledge.

It was written with prayers, tears, real-life stories, and deep conviction. It believes that knowing and using the power of Jesus's blood can change your life.

Whether you're a new believer, a seasoned Christian, or exploring faith, you'll find truths here. Truths that can transform your relationship with God and change your life.

Are you ready to discover the incredible power available to you through the blood of Jesus? Let's begin this fantastic journey together.

Turn the page. Let's explore how this ancient truth is critical to your success and vital for future breakthroughs.

Remember, this isn't just about learning – it's about experiencing.

My prayer is that by the time you finish this book, you'll never see the phrase "the blood of Jesus" the same way again.

Instead, you'll understand it as the dynamic, living power it is in your life today.

Let's begin.

Chapter 1: The Blood Covenant Throughout Scripture

Have you ever wondered why God chose blood for His relationship with humanity?

This fascinating journey starts in ancient history. It still affects us today.

Let me take you on an eye-opening exploration of this powerful truth.

The Ancient Power of Blood Covenants

IMAGINE LIVING IN ANCIENT times.

A promise was a matter of life and death. It wasn't just about signing papers. It was a blood-abiding promise.

Blood covenants were the most sacred agreements people could make. When two parties entered a blood covenant, they said, "My life for yours. What's mine is yours, and what's yours is mine."

Think about that for a moment.

These weren't casual agreements like we make today. They were unbreakable bonds that transformed strangers into family.

Here's what typically happens during a blood covenant ceremony:

- Both parties would make cuts in their wrists.
- They would let their blood flow together.
- They would exchange parts of their garments.
- They would state the terms of their covenant.

- They would share a memorial meal.
- They would exchange names.

Does that sound intense?

They meant it to be!

This ceremony said, "We're now closer than blood relatives. My life is now bound to yours."

God's First Blood Covenant: The Garden and Beyond

THE FIRST HINT OF BLOOD'S significance appears right after Adam and Eve's fall.

Remember those animal skins God used to clothe them? That required the first blood sacrifice in history. It wasn't just about covering their nakedness. By so doing, God said, "I'm making a way to restore our relationship."

Let's look at how this theme developed:

The Story of Abel's Offering

We often rush past this story, but it's crucial.

Why did God accept Abel's blood sacrifice but reject Cain's bloodless offering?

It wasn't about favourites. It was about God's demand for blood atonement. Abel got it. He understood that approaching God required a blood sacrifice.

Noah's Rainbow Covenant

After the flood, Noah's first act was to offer blood sacrifices. God responded with the first visible covenant sign—the rainbow. But this was just the beginning.

Abraham: The Covenant That Changed Everything

NOW, HERE'S WHERE IT gets fascinating.

God's covenant with Abraham was unlike anything before it. Picture this scene:

Abraham has split several animals in half, creating a path between them. He's waiting, probably wondering what's next.

Then, God Himself passes between the pieces. In a supernatural moment, He is a smoking furnace and a burning lamp.

What's happening here?

In those days, people made a covenant by walking between split animals. They said, "May this happen to me if I break this covenant?"

But in this case, only God walked through.

Why?

Because it was an unconditional covenant, it depended on His faithfulness, not Abraham's.

The Passover: A Picture of Things to Come

LET'S FAST-FORWARD to Egypt. God will deliver the Israelites, but they must first understand something crucial about blood.

God instructs them to place blood on their doorposts. This wasn't random – it was prophetic.

Every detail mattered:

- The lamb had to be perfect.
- The blood had to be applied.
- They had to remain under its covering.
- Death passed over where the blood was applied.

Sound familiar?

It should – it's a perfect picture of what Jesus would later do for us.

The Levitical System: God's Object Lesson

NOW, WE COME TO THE elaborate system of sacrifices God established.

Was God being demanding?

Not at all!

He was teaching His people vital truths about:

- The seriousness of sin.
- The necessity of blood atonement.
- The concept of substitution.
- The path to forgiveness and cleansing.

Consider these staggering stats. They sacrificed 22,000 cattle and 120,000 sheep and goats at Solomon's temple dedication!

Why so many?

Each sacrifice drove home the message: "Without blood, there is no forgiveness of sins."

The Day of Atonement: A Yearly Reminder

THE MOST SOLEMN DAY in Israel's calendar was Yom Kippur, the Day of Atonement. Every year, the High Priest would enter the Holy of Holies.

This yearly ritual pointed to something—or instead, Someone—greater to come.

Why Animal Blood Wasn't Enough

HERE'S THE THING ABOUT all these animal sacrifices—they were never meant to be the final solution.

They were like yearly credit card payments. They covered the debt but didn't pay it off. They were pointing to something better.

Think about it:

- The sacrifices had to be repeated.
- They only covered sins temporarily.
- They couldn't cleanse the conscience.
- They were limited in their effect.

This is why the prophets began speaking of a new covenant that would be different from all that came before.

Bringing It Home: Why This Matters Today

YOU MIGHT THINK, "THIS is interesting history, but what does it mean to me?"

Everything!

Understanding the blood covenant helps us:

- Grasp the significance of Jesus's sacrifice.
- Understand our position in Christ.
- Access our covenant rights and privileges.
- Walk in greater spiritual authority.
- Experience deeper intimacy with God.

Personal Reflection Time

TAKE A MOMENT TO CONSIDER:

1. How does knowing the history of blood covenants change your view of God's relationship with you?
2. What rights and privileges do you have as a covenant child of God?

3. How should this understanding affect your daily walk with God?

A Prayer of Response

FATHER, THANK YOU FOR helping me understand the profound significance of blood covenants. Thank You for not just making a contract with us—You made a covenant. Help me live in full awareness of what this means. In Jesus's name, Amen.

Looking Ahead

IN OUR NEXT CHAPTER, we'll see how Jesus fulfilled all the blood covenants.

Get ready – it's about to get even more exciting!

Remember: You're not just reading ancient history. You're finding your blood-bought inheritance in Christ.

Chapter 2: Jesus as the Perfect Sacrifice

Have you ever assembled a puzzle and found one piece that made the whole picture come together?

That's what Jesus's sacrifice did for all the blood covenants we discussed in Chapter 1.

Let's explore how Jesus became the perfect sacrifice that changed everything. It changed not just humanity but you personally.

When Heaven's Perfect Plan Unfolded

For thousands of years, countless animals have been sacrificed. Their blood was spilled on Jewish altars.

Yet, something was still missing. It was as if humanity was making payments on an infinite debt that could never be fully settled.

Then, at the right moment in history, God unveiled His master plan. It had been in the works since before time began.

The Prophecies: God's Preview of Coming Attractions

Let's see how, throughout history, God hinted at a coming perfect sacrifice.

Isaiah's Stunning Preview

SEVEN HUNDRED YEARS before Jesus, Isaiah wrote a prophecy so vivid it reads like a news report.

- "He was wounded for our transgressions."
- "By His stripes, we are healed"
- "The Lord has laid on Him the iniquity of us all" (Isaiah 53:3-5).

Isaiah described the crucifixion centuries before it came to pass!

Other Prophetic Voices

- David described the crucifixion in Psalms 22.
- Zechariah predicted the thirty pieces of silver.
- Daniel pinpointed the timeline.
- Micah named the birthplace.

IT'S LIKE GOD WAS SAYING, "Pay attention! Something incredible is coming!"

What Made Jesus's Blood Different?

NOW, HERE'S WHERE IT gets fascinating. Jesus's blood wasn't just ordinary human blood.

Let's break down what made it unique:

The Virgin Birth: A Divine Bloodline

Remember high school biology?

The mother's blood never mixes with the baby's blood. Jesus's blood came from a divine source. It was pure, not tainted by Adam's fallen nature. It was heaven's blood flowing through human veins!

Sinless Life: The Unblemished Lamb

Every other human being has sinned, making their blood impure for sacrifice.

But Jesus?

He lived 33 years without a single sin—not one wrong thought or selfish action.

Can you imagine that?

This made Him the only qualified candidate to be our sacrifice.

Divine and Human: The Perfect Mediator

Here's something mind-blowing: Jesus's blood contained divine and human properties.

He was:

- Fully God (so His sacrifice had infinite value).
- Fully human (so He could legally represent humanity).

It's like He built a bridge from both ends, connecting heaven and earth through His body.

The Day Heaven and Earth Stood Still

LET'S WALK THROUGH what happened on that crucial day:

The Last Supper: A New Covenant Introduced

Hours before His arrest, Jesus did something revolutionary.

He took the Passover cup and said, "This is my blood of the new covenant." He was instituting a new covenant while the old one was still in effect!

Gethsemane: The First Blood Shed

Before the crucifixion, Jesus sweated blood. It was a rare condition, hematidrosis, caused by extreme stress. From the very beginning, His sacrifice was unique.

The Medical Perspective of the Crucifixion

Warning: This section is graphic. But it's vital to know what Jesus endured:

- The scourging tore His flesh, exposing muscles and bones.
- The crown of thorns caused severe blood loss.
- The nails pierced significant blood vessels.
- The spear released the separated blood and water.

Every drop of bloodshed had a purpose. Every wound had meaning. It was well-spent.

The Spiritual Impact: What Actually Happened

WHILE HUMAN EYES SAW a brutal execution, a more remarkable event was happening in the spiritual realm.

The Exchange That Changed Everything

- He took our sins; we got His righteousness.
- He took our sickness; we got His health.
- He took our poverty; we got His abundance.
- He took our shame; we got His glory.
- He took our death; we got His life.

The Perfect Sacrifice Accepted

Remember how the High Priest would wait anxiously to see if God accepted the sacrifice?

The resurrection was God's thunderous "YES!" to Jesus's sacrifice. Jesus Christ paid the debt, and the work was finished.

Why Once Was Enough

UNLIKE THE OLD SYSTEM of repeated sacrifices, Jesus died once and for all.

Why?

Because His sacrifice was:

- Perfect in nature
- Infinite in value
- Eternal in effect
- Complete in scope.

Think about it: His one sacrifice covered:

- All people
- All sins

- All time
- All needs

Making It Personal: Your Response to the Perfect Sacrifice

THIS ISN'T JUST BEAUTIFUL theology – it's a life-changing truth that demands a response.

❧

HERE'S HOW TO MAKE it personal:

Accepting the Gift

Just as the Israelites had to apply the blood to their doorposts, we must accept and apply Christ's sacrifice to our lives.

It's not automatic – it requires our response.

Living in the Benefits

Once you understand what the perfect sacrifice accomplished, you can:

- Face guilt with confidence (It's covered!)
- Approach God boldly (The way is open!)
- Stand against the enemy (You're blood-bought!)
- Receive healing (By His stripes!)
- Walk in victory (It's finished!)

Practical Application Steps

1. Take a moment right now to thank Jesus specifically for His sacrifice.
2. Identify areas where you need to live in these benefits.
3. Begin declaring the power of the blood over your life daily.
4. Share this truth with someone who could benefit from

hearing it.

A Prayer of Gratitude and Acceptance

LORD JESUS, I AM OVERWHELMED by what You did for me. Thank You for being my perfect sacrifice. I accept everything You died to give me. Help me live each day with the full benefits of Your precious blood. Please show me how to share this amazing truth with others. In Your name, Amen.

Looking Forward

WE KNOW THE PERFECTION of Christ's sacrifice. Now, we can explore the seven-fold power of His blood in our lives today.

Get excited – the best is yet to come!

Remember: Every time you see a cross, let it remind you of Christ's death and the perfect sacrifice that made you accepted and ready for victory.

Chapter 3: Redemption Through the Blood

T hink about the most expensive purchase you've ever made.
A house?

A car?

Now imagine paying that price not for something but for someone.

That's what Jesus did through His blood. But His price was worth more than any money.

Let's discover what this means for you.

Understanding Biblical Redemption

LET ME PAINT A PICTURE that will help you grasp this powerful concept.

In ancient times, if someone couldn't pay their debts, they might be sold into slavery. The only way out was for someone to pay the redemption price – to buy their freedom. This person was called a "kinsman redeemer."

More Than Just a Religious Word

Redemption means:

- To buy back
- To pay the total price
- To release from bondage
- To restore to the original position
- To reclaim ownership.

It's like someone entering an auction house. They pay any price to buy back something precious that was lost.

The Price That Was Paid

WHAT WE LOST IN THE Fall
When Adam and Eve sinned, humanity lost:

- Intimate fellowship with God
- Divine authority over creation
- Spiritual and physical health
- Peace and security
- Eternal life.

WE BECAME SLAVES TO:

- Sin
- Satan
- Fear
- Death
- Corruption

The Cost of Our Freedom
The price wasn't gold or silver – it was the precious blood of Jesus.
Why blood?
Because:

- The source of life is in the blood (Leviticus 17:11).
- Sin requires a life payment.
- Only pure blood could cleanse impurity.
- Blood represents the ultimate price.

What Your Redemption Includes

HERE'S WHERE IT GETS exciting!

Your redemption package includes:

Freedom from Sin's Power

- No more bondage to old habits.
- Breaking of addictions
- Release from sinful patterns
- Power to say "no" to temptation.

Real-Life Story: Thulani's Victory

Let me tell you about Thulani, a man I counselled who struggled with addiction for 20 years. Everything changed when he finally understood the power of redemption through the blood. "It wasn't just willpower," he told me. "Something broke inside when I realized I was already bought and paid for."

Release from Satan's Authority

Jesus Christ has released you from Satan's bondage and all his cohorts. "And having disarmed the powers and authorities, he made a public spectacle of them, triumphing over them by the cross" (Col. 2:15).

Therefore, the devil has no legal right over you. You are guaranteed protection from evil.

You now have the authority to resist the enemy and are free from fear.

Breaking of Generational Curses

- Family patterns are broken.
- Inherited tendencies overcome.
- New spiritual DNA
- A fresh start for future generations

Restoration of Lost Inheritance

- Return to God's original plan
- Recovery of stolen blessings
- Restoration of divine purpose
- Reclaiming of destiny

The Legal Side of Redemption

THINK OF REDEMPTION like a divine court case:

- Satan was the prosecuting attorney.
- Sin was the evidence against us.
- The blood of Jesus paid our penalty.
- God declared, "Case dismissed!"

Your Legal Rights

Because of the blood, you now have:

- Right to forgiveness
- Right to healing
- Right to provision
- Right to protection
- Right to blessing.

Breaking Generational Patterns

ONE OF THE MOST POTENT aspects of redemption is its ability to break generational cycles.

Here's how it works:

Identifying Generational Issues

Look for:

- Repeated patterns in your family.

- Persistent struggles
- Common Weaknesses.
- "Family traits" that don't align with God's Word.

Applying the Blood

1. Acknowledge the pattern.
2. Renounce its power.
3. Declare your redemption.
4. Walk in the new authority.
5. Create new patterns.

Practical Steps to Walk in Redemption

KNOW YOUR RIGHTS

- Study what the blood has purchased.
- Understand your legal position.
- Learn your spiritual authority.
- Recognize your new identity.

Stand Your Ground

- Resist old patterns.
- Reject enemy accusations.
- Remember your redemption price.
- Reinforce your freedom daily.

Exercise Your Authority

- Speak redemption declarations.
- Apply the blood through prayer.
- Walk in your new identity.
- Help others find freedom.

Daily Redemption Declarations

START DECLARING THESE truths daily:

- "The blood of Jesus redeems me."
- "The price for my freedom has been paid in full."
- "No weapon formed against me shall prosper."
- "I am free from all bondage through the blood."
- "Generational curses are broken in my life."

Common Questions About Redemption

Q: "IF I'M REDEEMED, why struggle?"

A: Redemption is complete, but we grow in understanding and applying it. Like a paid-off house – it's entirely yours, but you need to live in it to enjoy it.

Q: "How do I maintain my freedom?"

A: Daily renew your mind, stand in faith, and apply the blood through declaration and praise.

Q: "What if I fall back into old patterns?"

A: Your redemption doesn't change. Return to the cross, receive forgiveness, and continue walking in freedom.

The Power of Testimonies

ANNE'S STORY

"For years, I lived under the shadow of my family's history of depression. Understanding redemption through the blood changed everything. I realized I didn't have to accept this 'inheritance.' Today, I walk in joy, and my children are growing up with a new legacy."

Your Personal Redemption Inventory

TAKE A MOMENT TO:

1. List areas where you need freedom
2. Write out what the blood says about each area
3. Create personal declarations of freedom
4. Plan specific steps to walk into your redemption

A Prayer of Redemption

PRECIOUS LORD, THANK You for paying the price for my complete redemption. I received everything. Your blood was purchased for me. I declare my freedom from every bondage, release from every curse, and right to walk in complete freedom. Help me live daily in the reality of my redemption. In Jesus' name, Amen.

Moving Forward

YOUR REDEMPTION IS a done deal – paid in full by the blood of Jesus. Now it's time to walk in it. Remember, you're not working for your freedom; you're working from your freedom.

Action Steps:

1. Read these redemption truths daily for the next 21 days
2. Share your redemption story with someone
3. Begin applying the blood specifically to areas of struggle
4. Join others who understand and walk in redemption

Remember: Every drop of Jesus's blood shouts "REDEEMED!" over your life. Live like it's true – because it is!

Coming Up Next: Chapter 4 will show how Jesus' blood justifies us before God. It gives us a new standing in His presence.

Chapter 4: Justification by the Blood

Have you ever wished you could start over with a spotless slate? Like having all your past mistakes, regrets, and failures wholly erased.

That's what justification through the blood of Jesus offers. But it's even better than you might imagine.

What Does Justification Mean?

LET ME BREAK THIS DOWN in a way that will revolutionize your understanding.

You know those times when you feel like you don't measure up? When guilt whispers that you're not good enough for God?

That's precisely what justification addresses.

More Than Just Forgiveness

Think of it this way:

- Forgiveness says, "Your debt is paid."
- Justification says, "It's like you never had a debt."

It's as if God checks your spiritual credit score. He clears all negative marks and gives you His perfect score!

The Divine Declaration

When God justifies you, He:

- Declares you righteous.
- Sees you as perfect in Christ.

- Treats you as if you'd never sinned.
- Gives you Jesus's standing with Him.
- Justification is an act of God the Father. He counts our sins as Christ's and Christ's righteousness as ours (2 Cor. 5:21).

The Legal Side Made Simple

LET ME USE A COURTROOM illustration that will help you with this click.

Picture yourself standing in God's courtroom:

- Satan is the accuser with a long list of charges.
- Your sins are the evidence against you.
- The penalty is eternal separation from God.
- You have no defence of your own.

But then something remarkable happens:

- Jesus steps forward as your advocate.
- He presents His blood as payment.
- The Judge (God) declares "NOT GUILTY!"
- You walk out legally righteous.

Personal Story: The Power of Understanding

I'll never forget counselling Angelina. She was a lifelong Christian but lived under constant condemnation.

Finally grasping justification, she cried, "You mean God doesn't just tolerate me? "He sees me as righteous?" That changed her view of God.

The Revolutionary Nature of Blood Justification

WHY BLOOD WAS REQUIRED

Have you ever wondered why blood was necessary?

Here's why:

- Sin requires a life payment.
- Only pure blood could satisfy justice.
- Jesus's blood was perfectly pure.
- His sacrifice was infinitely valuable.

The Complete Exchange
Through His blood, Jesus made a fantastic exchange:

- He took our sin → We got His righteousness
- He took our guilt → We got His innocence
- He took our shame → We got His honour
- He took our condemnation → We got His acceptance

Living in Your Justified Position

THE CHALLENGE MANY Face
Here's what I often hear: "But I still feel guilty..." "I keep remembering my past..." "I don't feel worthy..."
Sound familiar?
Let's address this head-on.
Understanding Feelings vs. Facts

- Feelings change → God's declaration doesn't.
- Emotions fluctuate → Your position remains stable.
- Memory accuses → Blood justifies.
- Satan condemns → Spirit confirms.

Practical Steps to Walk in Justification

RENEW YOUR MIND DAILY
Start your day declaring:

- "I am justified by the blood of Jesus."
- "God sees me as righteous in Christ."
- "I have peace with God through Jesus."
- "No accusation against me can stand."

Deal with Guilt Properly

When guilt comes:

1. Acknowledge the feeling
2. Check if it's conviction or condemnation
3. If you've sinned, confess it
4. Receive forgiveness immediately
5. Stand in your justified position
6. Answer the Accuser

When Satan brings up:

- Your past → Point to the blood
- Your failures → Declare your justification
- Your unworthiness → Stand in Christ's worthiness

The Benefits of Living Justified

CONFIDENCE WITH GOD

- No more hiding
- A bold approach to His throne
- Intimate fellowship
- Answered prayers

Emotional Freedom

- Release from shame
- Freedom from guilt

- Peace of mind
- Joy in relationship with God

Spiritual Authority

- Standing against the enemy
- Claiming promises
- Walking in victory
- Helping others find freedom

Common Questions About Justification

Q: "CAN I LOSE MY JUSTIFICATION if I sin?"

A: No! Your justification is based on Jesus's blood, not your performance. However, unconfessed sin can harm your fellowship with God. So, confess often.

Q: "How can God see me as righteous?"

A: Because He sees you through the blood of Jesus. It's not about pretending – it's about perfect substitution. Jesus's righteousness becomes yours.

Q: "What about when I feel unrighteous?"

A: Your feelings don't change God's declaration. Stand on what the blood says about you, not what your emotions say.

Justification in Daily Life

MAKING IT PRACTICAL

Apply your justified position to:

- Prayer time (approach confidently)
- Spiritual warfare (stand firmly)
- Ministry to others (serve boldly)
- Personal growth (learn securely)

Creating New Thought Patterns
Replace:

- "I'm not worthy" with "His blood justifies me."
- "God must be angry" with "I have peace with God."
- "I can't approach God" with "I have bold access."
- "I'm condemned" with "I'm completely justified."

Power Declarations of Justification

SPEAK THESE TRUTHS daily:

1. "I am justified by faith through the blood of Jesus."
2. "God sees me as righteous in Christ."
3. "No condemnation can stand against me."
4. "I have perfect standing with God."
5. "The blood speaks better things for me."

Your Justification Action Plan
Daily Steps:

1. Read the Word of God about justification.
2. Make declarations of your position.
3. Thank God for His gift of righteousness.
4. Walk confidently as justified.

Weekly Practice:

1. Share your understanding with others.
2. Review and celebrate victories.
3. Journal your growth in this truth.
4. Help someone else understand their position.

A Prayer of Recognition

HEAVENLY FATHER, THANK You for justifying me through the blood of Jesus. I receive this unique gift of righteousness. Help me walk in and completely understand what the blood has done. When guilt or condemnation comes, help me stand firm in my justified position. I am grateful that I can confidently come to You, knowing that I am fully accepted in Christ. *In Jesus's name, Amen.*

Looking Ahead

NOW THAT YOU KNOW YOUR justified position, you can learn how the blood sanctifies you daily.

Get ready. Chapter 5 will show you how to be holier while keeping your justified status!

Remember: When guilt whispers "guilty," Jesus' blood shouts "JUSTIFIED!" Live in that truth today.

Chapter 5: Sanctification Through the Blood

Have you ever watched a master artist restore a priceless painting? It's a fascinating process.

The initial cleaning reveals the basic image. Then, patient, detailed work begins to bring out the original beauty.

That's precisely how sanctification works in our lives through the blood of Jesus.

Understanding Sanctification: It's Not What You Think

LET'S CLEAR UP SOMETHING right away. Sanctification isn't about becoming a super-spiritual person who never has fun.

It's about becoming more authentically you – the person God designed you to be.

Sanctification is a gracious, ongoing work of the Holy Spirit. He frees the justified sinner from sin's pollution, renews his nature in God's image, and enables him to do good works.

Let's explore the dimensions of sanctification.

The Three Dimensions of Sanctification

Think of it like a beautiful diamond with three facets:

1. **Positional Sanctification**
    ○ Happened the moment you were saved.
    ○ You were set apart as God's own.

- ○ Complete and perfect in Christ.
- ○ Your new identity is established.

2. **Progressive Sanctification**
   - ○ Happening daily in your life.
   - ○ Growing in Christlikeness
   - ○ Learning to live from your new identity
   - ○ Becoming who you already are in Christ.

3. **Final Sanctification**
   - ○ It will happen when you see Jesus.
   - ○ Perfect transformation
   - ○ Complete resemblance to Christ.
   - ○ Your destiny is fulfilled.

⟡⟡⟡

The Blood's Role in Your Transformation

PERSONAL STORY: THE Garden Transformation

My neighbour Nikolai has this fantastic garden. When he first bought her house, the yard was messy – weeds everywhere, soil like concrete. But he didn't just clear the weeds (justification). He enriched the soil and kept working on it (sanctification). Today, it's a stunning display of flowers and fruits. That's exactly how the blood works in our lives.

How the Blood Sanctifies

The blood of Jesus:

- Cleanses continuously
- Transforms progressively
- Empowers consistently
- Renews constantly

Breaking Free from Performance-Based Holiness

HERE'S WHERE MANY BELIEVERS get stuck. They try to become holy through:

- Rigid rule-keeping
- Endless self-effort
- Strict religious practices
- Constant self-criticism

But true sanctification is different:

- It flows from the blood.
- It's empowered by grace.
- It's motivated by love.
- It's a natural growth process.

The Daily Process of Transformation

MORNING RECOGNITION

Start your day acknowledging:

- The blood already sanctifies you.
- The Holy Spirit is your helper.
- Growth is natural in God's presence.
- Today is an opportunity for transformation.

Moment-by-Moment Living

Practice these principles:

- Quick response to the Spirit's nudging.
- Immediate confession when you miss it.
- Constant awareness of the blood's cleansing.
- Regular declaration of your identity

Evening Reflection

Take time to:

- Celebrate areas of growth.
- Acknowledge areas needing change.
- Thank God for His patience.
- Rest in His continuing work.

Practical Steps for Growing in Holiness

MIND RENEWAL

Transform your thinking through:

- Scripture meditation
- Blood-based declarations
- Identity affirmations
- Truth-focused worship

Habit Formation

Develop holy habits through:

- Small, consistent choices
- Positive environment creation
- Accountability relationships
- Celebration of Progress

Character Development

Focus on growing in:

- Love
- Joy
- Peace
- Patience

- Kindness
- Goodness
- Faithfulness
- Gentleness
- Self-control

Dealing with Setbacks and Struggles

REAL-LIFE STORY: MICHAEL'S Journey

Michael came to me frustrated with his growth process. "I keep failing in the same areas," he shared. When we explored the power of sanctification through the blood, he realized he'd been trying to change using only willpower. Understanding the blood's continuous cleansing power revolutionized his approach to growth.

When You Stumble

Remember:

1. The blood hasn't stopped working.
2. Your identity has stayed the same.
3. Growth is still happening.
4. God isn't disappointed.
5. Keep moving forward.

The Role of the Holy Spirit

THINK OF IT THIS WAY:

- The blood provides cleansing.
- The Spirit provides the power.
- You give the cooperation.
- God provides the increase.

Breaking Stubborn Patterns

IDENTIFY THE ROOT
Look for:

- Underlying beliefs
- Hidden fears
- Past wounds
- False identities

Apply the Blood
Declare:

- "This pattern is broken by the blood."
- "I am being transformed."
- "Old things are passing away."
- "New life is flowing in me."

Creating an Environment for Growth

PHYSICAL ENVIRONMENT

- Surround yourself with truth.
- Create spaces for worship.
- Maintain order and peace.
- Remove unnecessary temptations.

Spiritual Environment

- Stay connected to believers.
- Maintain regular worship
- Keep short accounts with God.
- Practice gratitude

Emotional Environment

- Choose joy daily
- Process feelings honestly
- Maintain healthy boundaries
- Practice forgiveness quickly

Declarations for Transformation

START DECLARING:

1. "I am being transformed by the blood of Jesus."
2. "Holiness is my natural state in Christ."
3. "God's life is flowing through me."
4. "I am becoming more like Jesus daily."
5. "The blood is cleansing and changing me."

Your Growth Plan

DAILY PRACTICES

1. Morning blood declarations
2. Midday identity reminders
3. Evening gratitude and reflection
4. Continuous awareness of the blood's power

Weekly Rhythms

1. Deep Scripture meditation
2. Growth evaluation
3. Course corrections as needed
4. Celebration of Progress

Measuring True Growth

LOOK FOR:

- Increased love for others
- Greater peace in difficulties
- More consistent joy
- Growing spiritual hunger
- Natural resistance to sin

A Prayer for Continued Growth

FATHER, THANK YOU FOR the continuous cleansing and transforming power of the blood. Help me cooperate with Your work in my life. When I struggle, remind me that You're not frustrated with my process. I appreciate your patience as I grow. Help me see myself as You see me and become all You created me to be. In Jesus's name, Amen.

Looking Ahead

AS WE MOVE INTO CHAPTER 6, we'll discover how the blood provides healing for every area of our lives. Get ready – your understanding of divine health is about to expand!

Remember: Every drop of Jesus's blood carries transforming power. You're not just becoming holy – you're becoming more authentically you.

"But we all, with unveiled face, beholding as in a mirror the glory of the Lord, are being transformed into the same image from glory to glory." - 2 Corinthians 3:18

Chapter 6: Healing in the Blood

Have you noticed how a small paper cut triggers your body's healing response?

Within moments, your blood begins its miraculous work of healing and restoration.

The blood of Jesus has infinite power and heals all areas of life: physically, emotionally, mentally, and spiritually.

The Healing Power in His Blood

PERSONAL STORY: A DOCTOR'S Discovery

Dr Kraai, a friend and medical professional, once told me something fascinating. He said, "In all my years of practising medicine, I've never seen anything as remarkable as the human body's healing system in the blood."

"But, when I grasped the healing power in Jesus's blood, it changed how I viewed medicine and miracles."

Understanding Divine Health

It's more than just getting healed:

- It's God's original design for you.
- It's part of your redemption package.
- It's your blood bought right.
- It's available now through faith.

The Biblical Foundation for Healing

THE PROPHETIC PROMISE

"By His stripes, we are healed" wasn't just poetry. It was a promise that Jesus would fulfil physically.

Let's break down what happened:

1. Jesus was scourged (stripes placed on His back)
2. His blood was shed from those wounds
3. That blood purchased our healing
4. The price for health was paid in full.

In what areas does the blood affect your healing?

Four Dimensions of Blood-Bought Healing

PHYSICAL HEALING

- Disease and sickness
- Chronic conditions
- Injuries and wounds
- Genetic issues

Emotional Healing

- Past trauma
- Deep hurts
- Emotional wounds
- Relationship scars

Mental Healing

- Thought patterns
- Mental health

- Memory healing
- Cognitive restoration

Spiritual Healing

- Sin's damage
- Spiritual wounds
- Religious Trauma
- Inner brokenness

Real Stories of Blood-Bought Healing

NADIA'S STORY

Nadia had suffered from chronic pain for 15 years. "I had accepted it as my lot in life," she shared. "But when I understood that healing was in the blood of Jesus, something shifted. I began declaring my healing daily.

In three months, the pain that doctors said would never leave had vanished."

Michael's Journey

"My emotional wounds were deeper than any physical pain," Michael told me. "But understanding that Jesus's blood could heal my heart changed everything. The trauma that had haunted me for decades began to lose its power."

How to Receive Your Healing

KNOW YOUR RIGHTS

Remember:

- Healing has already been purchased
- It's part of your inheritance
- You don't have to earn it

- Jesus paid the total price

Position Yourself to Receive
Take these steps:

- Meditate on healing scriptures
- Declare your healing daily
- Thank God for health
- Rest in His finished work

Apply the Blood Through Faith
Practice:

- Speaking healing declarations
- Visualizing your healing
- Acting on your faith
- Maintaining gratitude

Overcoming Healing Hindrances

COMMON OBSTACLES

1. Doubt and Unbelief
   - Combat with God's Word
   - Focus on His faithfulness
   - Remember others' testimonies
   - Stand on His promises
2. Wrong Teaching
   - Study biblical healing
   - Reject religious traditions
   - Embrace truth fully
   - Share correct teaching
3. Past Disappointments

- Process honestly
- Release hurt
- Trust again
- Move forward in faith

Practical Steps for Walking in Health

DAILY HEALTH DECLARATION

Start your day declaring:

- "By His stripes, I am healed"
- "Divine health is my inheritance."
- "The life of God flows in my body."
- "Every cell in my body responds to His healing power."

Creating a Healing Environment

1. Physical Steps
   - Proper rest
   - Good nutrition
   - Regular exercise
   - Stress management
2. Spiritual Steps
   - Regular Worship
   - Word meditation
   - Prayer and communion
   - Faith declarations

When Healing Seems Delayed

REMEMBER:

- Hold onto your faith

- Keep declaring truth
- Stay in peace
- Trust God's timing
- Maintain hope

A Personal Note about Waiting
Sometimes, healing comes instantly; other times, it's progressive. Either way, you must believe in what the blood has purchased.

⚜

Ministering Healing to Others

BASIC PRINCIPLES

1. Share the truth about blood-bought healing.
2. Help build their faith through Scripture.
3. Pray with authority.
4. Encourage their ongoing faith.

Practical Steps

- Listen with compassion.
- Share relevant testimonies.
- Pray specifically
- Follow up with encouragement.

Special Focus: Emotional Healing

IDENTIFYING EMOTIONAL Wounds
Look for:

- Recurring emotional patterns
- Triggered responses

- Relationship difficulties
- Persistent fears

Applying the Blood
Declare over emotional areas:

- "The blood heals my emotions."
- "Past trauma loses its power."
- "My heart is being restored."
- "Peace replaces anxiety."

Healing Declarations

SPEAK THESE TRUTHS daily:

1. "The healing power in Jesus's blood flows through my body."
2. "Every cell, tissue, and organ functions in divine health."
3. "My emotions are healed and whole through the blood."
4. "My mind is renewed and restored by His power."
5. "I walk in complete wholeness – spirit, soul, and body."

Your Healing Action Plan

DAILY STEPS

1. Morning healing declarations
2. Thankfulness for health
3. Faith actions
4. Evening reflection

Weekly Practice

1. Study healing scriptures
2. Share testimonies

3. Minister to others
4. Celebrate progress

A Prayer for Healing Manifestation

PRECIOUS LORD, THANK You for purchasing my complete healing through Your blood. I receive everything. You died to give me. Let Your healing power flow through every part of my body, soul, and spirit. Help me walk in the fullness of divine health. Where I need specific healing, I trust Your power to make me whole. In Jesus's name, Amen.

Looking Ahead

Next, we'll explore how Jesus' blood protects every area of your life.

Get ready to discover the security that comes from being blood-covered!

Remember: Every drop of Jesus's blood carries healing power. Your part is to receive what He has already provided.

"He sent His word and healed them, and delivered them from their destructions." - Psalm 107:20

Chapter 7: Protection by the Blood

H ave you ever watched a mother bird spreading her wings over her nest during a storm?

There's something powerful about that picture of protection.

Now, imagine a cover that is infinitely more secure. That's what the blood of Jesus provides for you and your loved ones.

Understanding Your Blood Coverage

PERSONAL STORY: THE Storm That Changed Everything

I'll never forget the night a devastating tornado tore through our village. While a storm destroyed many homes, one family's testimony stood out.

Each morning, they prayed, applying Jesus's blood over their home. Their house stood untouched while others around it were severely damaged. "We weren't just lucky," they said. "We were blood-covered."

More Than Just Physical Protection

The blood provides:

- Spiritual protection
- Emotional security
- Mental safeguarding
- Physical safety
- Familial covering

The Passover Principle

LET'S LOOK AT THE ORIGINAL model of blood protection:

The First Passover

Remember what happened in Egypt?

Israel's houses had crimson blood marks on their doorposts. An angel of death swept above, passing silently. Within, families huddled securely.

The blood's power shielded all who trusted in it. It granted them sanctuary from doom.

All the households of Israel in Egypt were not harmed because of the covering of the blood.

Your Modern-Day Application

Just like then, the blood of Jesus still protects. The enemy must pass over you whenever the enemy attacks, for you are protected and guaranteed safety.

You activate your protection by faith.

Creating Your Blood-Protected Zone

YOUR PERSONAL SPACE

Cover daily:

- Your mind
- Your emotions
- Your body
- Your decisions
- Your future

1. Your Family Circle

Extend protection to:

- Spouse
- Children
- Parents
- Siblings
- Extended family

Your Property
Apply the blood over:

- Home
- Vehicles
- Workplace
- Possessions
- Investments

How to Apply the Blood

PRACTICAL STORY: MARCIA'S Method

Marcia, a single mother of three, developed a simple but powerful routine. "Every morning," she shares, "I walk through my home. I speak the blood of Jesus over each room, each child's bed, and every doorway."

Since starting this practice, we've experienced supernatural protection in countless situations."

❧

DAILY APPLICATION STEPS

1. Morning Declaration
   - Speak the blood over your day
   - Cover family members by name
   - Protect your environment
   - Declare divine safety
2. Throughout the Day

- ○ Quick reminders of coverage
- ○ Emergency applications
- ○ Thankful acknowledgement
- ○ Faith maintenance
3. Evening Reinforcement
   - ○ Review the day's protection
   - ○ Thank God for safety
   - ○ Cover the night hours
   - ○ Rest in security

Protection in Spiritual Warfare

UNDERSTANDING YOUR Position
You are:

- Blood-bought
- Blood-covered
- Blood-protected
- Blood-defended

Using Your Authority
When under attack:

1. Stand in your blood-bought position
2. Declare your protection
3. Resist the enemy
4. Maintain your peace

Specific Areas of Protection

MIND PROTECTION
Guard against:

- Negative thoughts
- Mental attacks
- Wrong beliefs
- Destructive patterns

Emotional Protection
Shield from:

- Toxic relationships
- Emotional manipulation
- Fear and anxiety
- Depression and despair

Physical Protection
Coverage for:

- Health and Safety
- Travel protection
- Accident prevention
- Disease resistance

Spiritual Protection
Defence against:

- Demonic attacks
- Spiritual deception
- False teachings
- Negative influences

Creating Protected Environments

YOUR HOME
Make it a sanctuary:

- Pray over each room
- Anoint entry points
- Declare the Word of God
- Maintain spiritual atmosphere

Your Workplace
Establish protection:

- Cover your space
- Protect relationships
- Guard decisions
- Maintain integrity

Your Travel
Secure your journeys:

- Pray before trips
- Cover vehicles
- Protect paths
- Ensure safe returns

Protection Declarations

START DECLARING:

1. "The blood of Jesus protects me."
2. "No weapon formed against me shall prosper."
3. "The blood secures my family."
4. "Evil must pass over my blood-covered life."
5. "I dwell in the secret place of the Most High."

Emergency Protection Protocol

WHEN FACING SUDDEN danger:

1. Immediately plead the blood
2. Stand in faith
3. Maintain peace
4. Trust God's protection
5. Take wise action

⚜

Teaching Children About Protection

AGE-APPROPRIATE METHODS

For young children:

- Simple prayers
- Basic understanding
- Safety consciousness
- Trust building

For older children:

- Deeper teaching
- Personal application
- Independent Practice
- Sharing with others

Maintaining Your Protection

DAILY HABITS

1. Morning coverage
2. Regular reinforcement
3. Evening securing
4. Continuous awareness

Weekly Practice

1. Family protection time
2. Property coverage
3. Extended family prayer
4. Testimony sharing

Testimonies of Protection

DAVID'S STORY

"I was driving home when a truck lost control and headed straight for me. In that split second, I declared, 'The blood of Jesus!' Somehow, the truck swerved around me without touching my car. The police officer said it was impossible, but I knew better."

The Springer Family "

Since we began applying the blood to our kids daily, we've seen fantastic protection. The difference is remarkable, from school challenges to peer pressure to physical safety."

Common Questions About Protection

Q: "DO I NEED TO APPLY the blood protection daily?"

A: Yes, like the Israelites needed fresh manna daily, we need a fresh application of the blood's protection.

Q: "What if I forget one day?"

A: God's love doesn't change. But daily protection prayers build your faith and awareness of His covering.

Q: "Can I protect others with the blood?"

A: You can pray for the blood's protection over loved ones. But they must choose their faith.

Your Protection Action Plan

Daily Steps

1. Morning protection ritual
2. Family coverage
3. Property protection
4. Travel safety
5. Emergency readiness

Creating Protection Habits

- Set regular times
- Use physical reminders
- Create family traditions
- Share testimonies

A Prayer of Protection

HEAVENLY FATHER, THANK You for the protecting power of Jesus's blood. I apply this blood covering every area of my life, family, and possessions. Thank You for Your divine security system that never fails. Help me walk in the consciousness of this protection daily. In Jesus's name, Amen.

Looking Ahead

IN OUR NEXT CHAPTER, we'll explore how the blood gives us access to God's presence.

Get ready to discover the closeness to you through Jesus' blood!

Remember: Every drop of Jesus's blood declares "Protected!" over your life. Live confidently in that divine security today.

"When I see the blood, I will pass over you." - Exodus 12:13

Chapter 8: Access Through the Blood

Imagine standing outside the most exclusive venue in the world. A long line of people is waiting, hoping somehow to gain entrance.

But you have something special – an all-access pass that lets you walk right in through the front door.

That's what the blood of Jesus provides. It gives us unlimited access to God's presence.

The Revolutionary Access We Now Have

PERSONAL STORY: THE President's Son

A friend once told me about meeting the President's son at a conference. "What struck me," he said, "wasn't just that he had access to the Presidential House. It was how naturally he walked in that access." He didn't have to think about it – it was simply his reality as a son." That's the kind of access the blood of Jesus gives us to God's throne.

From Distance to Intimacy

Think about the transformation of what has transpired.

In the Old Testament, only the High Priest had access to enter the Holy of Holies once a year.

Thanks to Jesus Christ's sacrifice on the cross, every believer can access the throne of glory anytime.

Before Jesus Christ shed blood, access to God was only through a human priest.

However, now all believers have direct access through Jesus Christ.

Understanding Your Blood-Bought Access

NOW THAT JESUS CHRIST'S blood has bought access for you, you have a direct approach to God.

Your access to Him is not limited; you have 24/7 access to the throne.

As His child, you have a close bond with the Father. You are confident in His presence because of the complete reconciliation you received through Christ.

The Veil is Torn

VISUAL IMPACT: THE Temple Moment

Picture that dramatic moment when Jesus died. The massive temple veil, thick as a man's hand, was supernaturally torn from top to bottom. God was making a statement: "The way is now open!"

What This Means for You

What a privilege you've received in Him.

There's no more separation; the reconciliation bridge has been set. Therefore, there is no need for human mediators and no waiting period.

No religious rituals are required to access and have intimate fellowship with God. To be saved, you need only believe in Jesus Christ as your Lord and Savior and be purified by Him. That's the only qualification.

Practical Steps to Exercise Your Access

MORNING ACCESS

Start your day with:

- Conscious entry into His presence
- Thank you for the blood's provision

- Enjoyment of fellowship
- Receiving daily grace

Throughout the Day
Practice:

- Quick connections
- Instant fellowship
- Continuous communion
- Natural dialogue

Special Moments
Set aside time for:

- Deep worship
- Extended prayer
- Intimate fellowship
- Spiritual renewal

Breaking Down Access Barriers

COMMON HINDRANCES

1. Feeling Unworthy
   - Remember: It's about His blood, not your performance
   - Access is your birthright
   - Worthiness comes through Jesus
   - Stand in His finished work
2. Religious Mindsets
   - Let go of old patterns
   - Embrace direct relationship
   - Trust His welcome

    ○ Walk in freedom

3. Past Experiences
    ○ Heal from religious trauma
    ○ Embrace Father's love
    ○ Build new patterns
    ○ Create fresh memories

Living in Open Access

DAILY RECOGNITION

Remember:

- You are welcome in His presence
- Access is always available
- Fellowship is natural
- Intimacy is normal

Building Confidence

Practice:

- Bold approach
- Regular fellowship
- Honest communication
- Relaxed communion

The Benefits of Unlimited Access

SPIRITUAL BENEFITS

- Constant guidance
- Divine wisdom
- Spiritual growth
- Increased revelation

Emotional Benefits

- Deep peace
- Lasting joy
- Emotional healing
- Inner security

Practical Benefits

- Clear direction
- Divine timing
- Supernatural help
- Heaven's resources

Making the Most of Your Access

CREATING SACRED SPACES

Designate:

- Prayer corners
- Worship times
- Quiet moments
- Fellowship opportunities

Developing Access Habits

Practice:

- Morning entry
- Midday check-ins
- Evening reflection
- Continuous awareness

Access in Different Seasons

IN TIMES OF JOY

- Share your happiness
- Express gratitude
- Celebrate together
- Deepen intimacy

In Times of Crisis

- Run to His presence
- Find refuge
- Receive comfort
- Access help

In Daily Routine

- Walk in fellowship
- Share thoughts
- Seek guidance
- Enjoy communion

Teaching Others About Access

HELPING OTHERS UNDERSTAND

Share:

- Your experiences
- Simple truths
- Practical steps
- Personal testimonies

Building Corporate Access

Create:

- Group experiences
- Shared moments
- Community Worship
- Collective prayer

Access Declarations

SPEAK THESE TRUTHS:

1. "I have bold access through the blood."
2. "God's presence is my home."
3. "I approach God with confidence."
4. "The way is always open for me."
5. "I live in continuous fellowship."

Your Access Action Plan

DAILY STEPS

1. Morning entrance
2. Midday connection
3. Evening fellowship
4. Continuous awareness

Weekly Practice

1. Extended communion
2. Deep worship
3. Focused prayer
4. Shared fellowship

Real-Life Stories of Access

SUZANNE'S JOURNEY

"I used to think I needed to 'clean up my act' before approaching God. Understanding blood-bought access changed everything. Now I come just as I am, knowing His blood has made the way."

Pastor Tom's Discovery

"After 20 years in ministry, I finally understood. It's not about religious activity; it's about blood-bought access." This revolutionized my personal life and my entire approach to ministry."

Special Focus: Crisis Access

WHEN TROUBLE HITS:

1. Run immediately to His presence.
2. Trust your access rights.
3. Receive His peace.
4. Access His wisdom.
5. Stand in confidence.

A Prayer of Access Recognition

FATHER, THANK YOU FOR the unique access I have through the blood of Jesus. Help me live daily in the reality of this open door to Your presence. When I'm tempted to stay away, remind me that the way is always open. Thank You for making me welcome in Your presence. In Jesus's name, Amen.

Looking Ahead

IN OUR NEXT CHAPTER, we'll explore how the blood of Jesus gives us victory in every area of life. Get ready to discover the triumph that's yours through His blood!

Remember: Every drop of Jesus's blood declares "Welcome!" over your life. The door is open – come on in!

"Let us therefore come boldly to the throne of grace, that we may obtain mercy and find grace to help in time of need." - Hebrews 4:16

Chapter 9: Victory Through the Blood

Have you ever watched a sports team that couldn't lose?

There's something powerful about knowing the outcome before the game even starts.

That's what the blood of Jesus provides. It guarantees victory in every battle you face.

Understanding Your Victory Position

PERSONAL STORY: THE Champion's Mindset

I'll never forget watching my friend Marcus coach his son's first boxing match. Before the fight, he told his son, "Son, you've already won in training. Now, go live out that victory."

We should approach life through the blood of Jesus. We're not fighting for victory; we're fighting for victory.

The Difference Between Fighting for and From Victory

Let me tabulate the reasoning for a better understanding.

- Fighting For: Uncertain outcome
- Fighting From: Already settled
- Fighting For: Depends on your strength
- Fighting From: Rests on His finished work

Your Blood-Bought Victory Rights

WHAT JESUS SECURED

Victory over Sin

The blood of Jesus enables you to break from bad habits and frees you from any bondage.

Though temptations will come, you've power over them. Temptations have no hold on you. The battle has been won.

Victory over Satan

In his letter to the Colossians, Paul says the powers and authorities have been disarmed. The fight is over!

Sin has no domination over you (Rom. 6:14), and you have complete triumph.

Victory over Circumstances

Your blood-bought victory gives you the right to financial breakthroughs and career advancement.

Your relationships are restored on all levels.

Health wholeness is part of you.

Living from Victory, Not Toward It

REAL-LIFE VICTORY STORY: Buhle's Breakthrough

Buhle had struggled with anxiety for decades. "I kept trying to fight my way to victory," she shared. "Everything changed when I realized I wasn't fighting for victory – the blood had already won it. Now I stand in that victory when anxiety tries to come."

Practical Victory Steps

1. Start Your Day in Victory
    ◦ Declare your position.
    ◦ Thank God for triumph.
    ◦ Walk in confidence.
    ◦ Expect success
2. Face Challenges Victoriously
    ◦ Remember your standing.
    ◦ Apply the blood.
    ◦ Stand firm

○ Watch God work.

Overcoming Common Victory Stealers

PAST DEFEATS

Counter with:

- Blood-bought victory
- New identity
- Fresh start
- Present triumph

Current Struggles

Remember:

- Victory is already yours.
- Circumstances don't define the outcome.
- Stand in faith
- Maintain peace

Future Fears

Know that His blood covers tomorrow. Your victory is guaranteed. Why?

Because God has assured you of success, and He always goes before you.

Victory in Specific Areas

FINANCIAL VICTORY

You are free from debt, have plenty, and live generously. It's all thanks to Jesus' bloody victory.

He also gives you insight into wise stewardship.

Relationship Victory

- Restored connections
- Healed hurts
- Strong bonds
- Peaceful interactions

Health Victory

- Physical wellness
- Emotional health
- Mental clarity
- Spiritual vitality

Career Victory

- Divine favour
- Strategic advancement
- Purposeful work
- Impactful service

Maintaining Your Victory Stance
Daily Victory Practices

1. Morning Victory Declaration
   - Speak victory words.
   - Claim promises
   - Thank you for your triumph.
   - Walk confidently
2. Mid-Day Victory Check
   - Assess stance
   - Adjust if needed
   - Reinforce truth
   - Continue strong
3. Evening Victory Review

- ○ Celebrate wins
- ○ Learn from challenges
- ○ Rest in victory
- ○ Prepare for tomorrow

Victory Declarations

SPEAK THESE DAILY:

1. "I am more than a conqueror through the blood."
2. "Victory is my inheritance in Christ."
3. "No weapon formed against me prospers."
4. "I walk in triumph through the blood."
5. "Success is my portion in Jesus."

Teaching Others About Victory

SHARING VICTORY PRINCIPLES

- Your testimony
- Biblical examples
- Practical applications
- Living proof

Helping Others Stand

- Encourage faith
- Share wisdom
- Provide support
- Celebrate wins

Victory in Spiritual Warfare

USING YOUR AUTHORITY

1. Stand in Position
   - Know your place
   - Maintain ground
   - Exercise authority
   - Expect results
2. Wield Your Weapons
   - The blood
   - God's Word
   - Prayer
   - Faith

Victory Stories That Inspire

THE BUSINESS BREAKTHROUGH

"Our company was facing bankruptcy. Once we knew victory through the blood, we declared it daily over our business. Within six months, we had our most profitable season ever."

The Marriage Restoration

"Everyone said our marriage was over. But standing in blood-bought victory, we saw God restore what seemed impossible. Today, we're stronger than ever."

Practical Victory Tools

VICTORY JOURNAL
Record:

- Daily victories
- Breakthrough moments
- Learning experiences

- Gratitude points

Victory Partners
Connect with:

- Prayer partners
- Accountability friends
- Mentors
- Support group

Special Focus: Victory in Crisis

WHEN TROUBLES COME:

1. Remember your position
2. Stand in the blood
3. Declare victory
4. Maintain peace
5. Watch God work

Victory Mindset Training

RENEWING YOUR MIND
Replace:

- Defeat with victory
- Fear with faith
- Doubt with confidence
- Worry with trust

Building Victory Habits
Develop:

- Regular declarations

- Consistent prayer
- Word meditation
- Faith actions

Your Victory Action Plan

DAILY STEPS

1. Morning victory stance
2. Midday victory check
3. Evening victory review
4. Continuous victory awareness

Weekly Practice

1. Victory celebration
2. Strategy review
3. Testimony sharing
4. Future planning

A Prayer of Victory

LORD JESUS, THANK YOU for securing my victory through Your blood. I choose to stand in this triumph today. When challenges come, help me remember that the battle is already won. Thank You for making me more than a conqueror. In Your mighty name, Amen.

Looking Ahead

IN PART 3, WE'LL EXPLORE how to use these blood-bought truths daily. Get ready to discover how to walk out your victory in every situation!

Remember: Every drop of Jesus's blood shouts "VICTORY!" over your life. Live today like the champion you are in Him!

"But thanks be to God, who gives us the victory through our Lord Jesus Christ." - 1 Corinthians 15:57

Chapter 10: Pleading the Blood

Have you ever held a blank check signed by a millionaire? It's like pleading for Jesus's blood. It accesses an infinite account of spiritual power and provision.

However, many believers need help understanding this practice or are unsure how to do it well. Let's change that today.

What Does "Pleading the Blood" Really Mean?

PERSONAL STORY: A LAWYER'S Insight

My friend Dali, a veteran attorney, gave me a powerful perspective on this. "When I plead a case," he said, "I'm not begging the court. I'm presenting legal evidence and claiming rights based on established law."

That's what pleading the blood is about. It's a legal claim to what Jesus has purchased for you.

More Than Just Words

It's not:

- A magical formula
- Religious repetition
- Desperate begging
- Spiritual manipulation

It is:

- Legal declaration
- Faith activation

- Authority exercise
- Covenant claiming

The Biblical Basis for Pleading the Blood

OLD TESTAMENT FOUNDATIONS

Look at these examples:

- Abel's blood spoke (Genesis 4:10)
- Passover blood protected (Exodus 12)
- Sacrifice blood atoned (Leviticus 17:11)
- Covenant blood sealed (Exodus 24:8)

New Testament Fulfilment

See how it developed:

- Jesus's blood speaks better things (Hebrews 12:24)
- Overcomes the accuser (Revelation 12:11)
- Provides ongoing cleansing (1 John 1:7)
- Maintains our covenant (Hebrews 13:20)

When to Plead the Blood
In Times of Spiritual Warfare

- Against demonic attacks.
- For mental peace.
- Over spiritual atmosphere.
- During intense battles.

For Protection

- Over your family
- Around your property
- During travel

- In dangerous situations

For Provision

- Financial needs
- Resource requirements
- Business dealings
- Career matters

For Healing

- Physical ailments
- Emotional wounds
- Mental struggles
- Relationship healing

How to Plead the Blood Effectively

REAL-LIFE EXAMPLE: Dinah's Method

Dinah faced a severe threat to her children's safety at school.

Here's what she did:

"Every morning, I would walk around their beds while they slept, pleading the blood of Jesus."

I declared, "This blood protects my children from all evil." The results were remarkable. Her children remained safe despite several dangers at their school.

Step-by-Step Guide

1. Start with Recognition
   - Know what the blood purchased
   - Understand your rights
   - Acknowledge its power
   - Stand in faith

2. Make Your Declaration
    ◦ Speak with authority
    ◦ Be specific
    ◦ Stand confident
    ◦ Maintain faith
3. Stand in Victory
    ◦ Hold your ground
    ◦ Expect results
    ◦ Thank God in advance
    ◦ Walk in peace

Common Mistakes to Avoid

EMPTY REPETITION
Instead:

- Speak with understanding.
- Declare with faith.
- Mean what you say.
- Expect results.

Desperate Pleading
Remember:

- You're claiming rights.
- Not begging God.
- Standing in authority
- Accessing provision

Inconsistency
Practice:

- Regular application

- Persistent faith
- Continuous awareness
- Steady declaration

Practical Applications in Daily Life

MORNING ROUTINE

Start your day:

- Personal covering
- Family protection
- Daily provision
- Divine guidance

Throughout the Day

Maintain coverage:

- Quick reminders
- Instant application
- Continuous awareness
- Faith declarations

Evening Practice

End your day:

- Review coverage
- Reinforce protection
- Rest in security
- Thank for results

Teaching Your Family

FOR CHILDREN
Make it simple:

- Use illustrations
- Tell stories
- Practice together
- Celebrate results

For Teens
Help them understand:

- Personal application
- Practical use
- Power available
- Protection provided

Special Situations

CRISIS RESPONSE
When trouble hits:

1. Immediately plead the blood
2. Stand in faith
3. Maintain peace
4. Expect victory
5. Watch God work

Preventive Application
Before challenges:

- Create blood covering
- Establish protection

- Build faith walls
- Maintain guard

Power Declarations for Pleading the Blood

FOR PROTECTION

"Through the blood of Jesus, I declare:

- A shield of protection around me.
- A hedge of safety for my family.
- Divine coverage over my property.
- Complete security in all areas."

For Provision

"By the blood of Jesus, I claim:

- All my needs were met
- Resources released
- Abundance flowing
- Provision manifested"

For Healing

"Through the blood of Jesus, I receive:

- Complete healing
- Total Restoration
- Perfect health
- Abundant life"

Your Daily Pleading Practice

MORNING DECLARATION

"I apply the blood of Jesus over:

1. My mind, will, and emotions.
2. My body, health, and strength.
3. My family and relationships.
4. My work and ministry.
5. My property and possessions."

Specific Situation Guide
Create personalized declarations for:

- Your unique needs
- Family situations
- Work challenges
- Ministry opportunities

A Prayer of Application

DEAR LORD JESUS, WANT to thank You for Your precious blood. *I choose to activate its power in my life today. Help me understand more deeply how to plead Your blood effectively. Let every declaration be filled with faith and power. In Your mighty name, Amen.*

Looking Ahead

IN OUR NEXT CHAPTER, we'll explore how to incorporate the blood into our worship and prayer life. Get ready to discover new dimensions of power in your spiritual practices!

Remember: You activate heaven's power on earth whenever you plead the blood. Use this authority wisely and consistently!

"And they overcame him by the blood of the Lamb and by the word of their testimony." - Revelation 12:11

Chapter 11: The Blood in Worship and Prayer

Have you noticed that some songs or prayers reach the heavens while others bounce off the ceiling?

Knowing the role of blood in worship and prayer can transform your spiritual experience from routine to revolutionary.

The Power of Blood-Based Worship

PERSONAL STORY: A WORSHIP Leader's Discovery

A worship leader I know, Asiphe, shared something fascinating. "For years, I led worship focusing on music quality and song selection."

Then I discovered the power of blood in worship. Everything changed. It wasn't about performance anymore—it became about presence."

Why the Blood Matters in Worship

It's because:

- The blood gives us access
- It cleanses our worship
- It makes our praise acceptable
- It removes all barriers

Transforming Your Prayer Life

THE BLOOD AS YOUR PRAYER Foundation

Think of it this way:

- It's like having a VIP pass
- Opens direct communication
- Ensures God's attention
- Guarantees acceptance

Blood-Enhanced Prayer Patterns

STARTING YOUR PRAYER Time
Begin by acknowledging:

- The blood's cleansing
- Your right to approach
- God's welcoming presence
- Your accepted position

During Prayer
Remember to:

- Stand in blood authority
- Claim blood-bought promises
- Trust in your acceptance
- Rest in His presence

Closing Prayer
End with:

- Gratitude for access
- Faith in answers
- Confidence in acceptance
- Peace in His presence

Worship Songs About the Blood

TRADITIONAL HYMNS

Powerful classics like:

- "Nothing but the Blood"
- "There is Power in the Blood"
- "Are You Washed in the Blood?"
- "The Blood Will Never Lose Its Power"

Why They Still Matter
These songs carry:

- Deep theological truth
- Tested testimonies
- Generational power
- Timeless wisdom

Contemporary Songs
Modern expressions like:

- "The Blood of Jesus Speaks"
- "Nothing But the Blood" (modern version)
- "Thank You for the Blood"
- "The Power of the Blood"

Creating Blood-Conscious Worship

PERSONAL WORSHIP TIME
Include:

1. Blood acknowledgement
2. Gratitude expressions
3. Victory declarations
4. Intimate fellowship

Corporate Worship

Incorporate:

1. Blood-focused songs
2. Communion celebrations
3. Blood testimonies
4. Victory declarations

The Blood in Different Prayer Types

INTERCESSION

Apply the blood over:

- People you're praying for
- Situations you're addressing
- Nations you're covering
- Churches you're supporting

Warfare Prayer

Use the blood for:

- Breaking strongholds
- Defeating enemies
- Claiming territory
- Establishing victory

Personal Petitions

Present requests through:

- Blood-bought rights
- Covenant promises
- Legal standing
- Faith access

Special Focus: Communion and Prayer

MAKING COMMUNION MEANINGFUL
Remember:

- It's more than a ritual
- It's covenant renewal
- It's power activation
- It's an intimate fellowship

Personal Communion Time
Create special moments:
Set sacred space

1. Prepare your heart
2. Remember His sacrifice
3. Receive His life

Prayer Patterns Using the Blood

MORNING PRAYER PATTERN
"Lord, through Your blood:

1. I enter Your presence
2. I claim Your promises
3. I receive Your life
4. I walk in victory."

Warfare Prayer Pattern
"By the blood of Jesus:

1. I break every stronghold
2. I defeat every enemy
3. I claim every promise

4. I walk in triumph."

Fasting and the Blood Covenant

ENHANCING YOUR FAST
Remember:

- The blood empowers your fast
- It cleanses your sacrifice
- It ensures acceptance
- It brings breakthrough

Fasting Declarations
Speak forth:

1. "The blood sanctifies this fast."
2. "My sacrifice is accepted through the blood."
3. "Breakthrough comes by the blood."
4. "Victory is assured in the blood."

Corporate Worship Experiences

LEADING BLOOD-CONSCIOUS Worship
Guide people to:

1. Understand the blood's power
2. Enter with confidence
3. Worship in freedom
4. Experience His presence

Creating Atmosphere
Develop:

- Reverent awareness

- Grateful recognition
- Powerful declaration
- Intimate worship

Practical Prayer Applications

DAILY PRAYER LIST
Include:

- Blood acknowledgement
- Covenant claims
- Victory declarations
- Grateful recognition

Prayer Journal
Record:

- Blood revelations
- Answered prayers
- Victory testimonies
- Growth insights

Teaching Others About Blood-Based Prayer

SIMPLE STEPS FOR BEGINNERS
Help them:

1. Understand the basics
2. Start simple practices
3. Build confidence
4. Experience victory

Advanced Training
Guide in:

1. Deeper understanding
2. Powerful application
3. Effective ministry
4. Leadership development

A Model Prayer Using the Blood

"HEAVENLY FATHER, I come to You through the precious blood of Jesus. Thank You for this blood-bought access to Your throne. I stand before You cleansed and accepted. Let my worship rise as a sweet fragrance, And my prayers reach Your heart. Through the blood of Jesus, Amen."

Blood-Based Worship Declaration
"Through the blood of Jesus:

- I enter Your courts with praise
- I approach Your throne with confidence
- I worship in spirit and truth
- I commune with You in intimacy."

Your Worship and Prayer Action Plan

DAILY PRACTICE

1. Morning blood acknowledgement
2. Midday communion
3. Evening thanksgiving
4. Continuous awareness

Weekly Rhythm

1. Extended worship time
2. Communion celebration
3. Prayer partnership

4. Victory testimony

Looking Ahead

OUR NEXT CHAPTER WILL explore how to live daily under the blood covenant. Get ready to discover how this understanding transforms every aspect of your life!

Remember: Prayers and songs about the blood have extraordinary power. Let this truth revolutionize your spiritual life!

"Let us therefore come boldly to the throne of grace, that we may obtain mercy and find grace to help in time of need." - Hebrews 4:16

Chapter 12: Living Under the Blood Covenant

I magine having unlimited access to the wealthiest person's resources but never using them.

That's what many believers do with their blood covenant rights.

Today, we'll change that. We'll learn to live every moment with the full benefits of this fantastic covenant.

Understanding Your Covenant Position

PERSONAL STORY: THE Adoption Papers

I'll always remember watching my friends complete their adoption of little Zozo. The moment the judge signed those papers, everything changed.

Zozo instantly had all a natural-born child's rights, privileges, and inheritance. That's what the blood covenant does for us – it makes us legal heirs of everything God has!

Your New Identity

You are a covenant child; all that belongs to God is yours.

The apostle Paul writes to the Romans, "If we are children, then we are heirs of God and co-heirs with Christ." Through the blood of Jesus, you are in the new covenant, which is better than the old one.

Remember, you are a chosen people, a royal priesthood, a holy nation, a people belonging to God (1 Peter 29).

God is now your father.

Daily Blood Covenant Living

MORNING RECOGNITION

Start your day acknowledging:

1. Who you are in the covenant.
2. What's available to you
3. How to access it
4. Where to apply it

Real-Life Example: Dan's Morning Routine

"Every morning before work," Dan shares, "I spend five minutes declaring my rights." It's changed how I face each day. Problems that used to overwhelm me now look different through covenant eyes."

Throughout Your Day

Remember to:

- Walk in covenant awareness.
- Access covenant benefits.
- Claim covenant promises.
- Share covenant blessings.

Practical Benefits of Covenant Living

IN YOUR PERSONAL LIFE

Covenant living gives you access to Divine wisdom and supernatural peace. Through grace, you acquire peace and love that are beyond understanding.

Your joy becomes your strength, and the Almighty God is your life compass.

In Your Family

Experience:

- Protected relationships
- Blessed children
- Harmonious home
- Generational impact

In Your Work
Enjoy:

- Divine favour
- Supernatural provision
- Strategic wisdom
- Abundant success

Making It Personal: Your Covenant Checklist

DAILY COVENANT ACTIVATION
✓ Morning Declaration

- "I am in blood covenant with Almighty God."
- "Every covenant promise is mine today."
- "I walk in covenant authority."
- "I access the covenant provision."

Covenant Consciousness
Remember:

- You're never alone.
- Resources are available.
- Help is guaranteed.
- Victory is assured.

Maintain this covenant consciousness in your life.

Building a Covenant Family

TEACHING YOUR CHILDREN

Help them understand:

1. Their covenant identity
2. Their covenant rights
3. Their covenant responsibilities
4. Their covenant inheritance

Creating Covenant Traditions

Establish:

- Family communion times
- Covenant celebrations
- Blessing declarations
- Victory sharing

Covenant Benefits in Every Area

HEALTH AND HEALING

As an heir of heavenly things, claim your divine health and quick recovery. Know that you have strong immunity against all diseases because of who you are.

However, this doesn't mean you should eat junk food and pollute the temple of God.

Your health and healing come when you live in the grace of God.

Financial Provision

Access:

- Supernatural supply
- Wise stewardship
- Abundant resources

- Generous living

⸙

RELATIONSHIP BLESSINGS

Experience:

- Restored connections
- Healed hearts
- Strong bonds
- Peaceful interactions

Overcoming Covenant Challenges

When Facing Doubts

Remember:

1. It's based on his faithfulness.
2. It's sealed with blood.
3. It's legally binding.
4. It's eternally secure.

When Results Seem Delayed

Stand firm:

- Review covenant promises.
- Maintain faith declarations.
- Stay in peace.
- Expect manifestation.

Special Focus: Covenant Decision-Making

Major Decisions

Consider:

1. Covenant perspective

2. Covenant promises
3. Covenant guidance
4. Covenant provision

Daily Choices
Ask:

- Does this align with the covenant?
- Will this strengthen the covenant?
- How does covenant apply?
- What's the covenant solution?

Covenant Business Principles
Operating in Covenant
Apply:

- Integrity in dealings
- Excellence in service
- Wisdom in decisions
- Faith in provision

Covenant Workplace
Create:

- Positive atmosphere
- Fair treatment
- Honest practices
- Blessed environment

Your Covenant Declaration List
Personal Declarations
"Through the blood covenant:

1. I am blessed and highly favoured.
2. I walk in divine health.
3. I prosper in all things.
4. I succeed in every endeavour.

Family Declarations

"By covenant power:

1. My family is protected.
2. My children are blessed.
3. My marriage is strong.
4. My home is peaceful.

<hr>

Living from Covenant Abundance

MINDSET SHIFT

From:

- Survival to abundance
- Lack to provision
- Fear to faith
- Doubt to certainty

To:

- Expecting good
- Claiming provision
- Walking in authority
- Living in victory

Practical Covenant Applications

DAILY LIFE SITUATIONS
Apply covenant to:

- Work challenges
- Family needs
- Health issues
- Financial matters

Emergency Response
In crisis:

1. Remember covenant position
2. Declare covenant rights
3. Access covenant help
4. Rest in covenant care

Teaching Others About Covenant Living
Simple Explanations
Share:

- Basic principles
- Personal testimonies
- Practical applications
- Real results

Mentoring Others
Guide in:

- Understanding rights
- Accessing benefits
- Walking in authority
- Living victoriously

Your Covenant Action Plan

DAILY STEPS

1. Morning covenant review
2. Midday covenant check
3. Evening covenant gratitude
4. Continuous covenant awareness

Weekly Practice

1. Deeper covenant study
2. Family covenant time
3. Covenant Celebration
4. Testimony sharing

A Covenant Prayer

"HEAVENLY FATHER, THANK You for making me a covenant child through the blood of Jesus. Help me live today with full awareness and benefit from this amazing relationship. Let every step I take be a reflection of my covenant position. In Jesus' name, Amen."

Looking Ahead

IN PART 4, WE'LL EXPLORE uses of the blood in spiritual warfare, healing, and deliverance. Get ready to see how your covenant position empowers you for effective ministry!

Remember: Every moment of every day, you're living under the most powerful covenant ever made – sealed by the precious blood of Jesus. Live like it's true because it is!

"Now may the God of peace who brought up our Lord Jesus from the dead, that great Shepherd of the sheep, through the blood of the everlasting

covenant, make you complete in every good work to do His will." - Hebrews 13:20-21

Chapter 13: The Blood in Spiritual Warfare

Have you ever watched a skilled martial artist who knows how to use their weapons? There's a confidence that comes with that knowledge.

In spiritual battles, the blood of Jesus is your most potent weapon. But, like any weapon, you must know how to use it.

Understanding Your Battle Position

PERSONAL STORY: THE Veteran's Wisdom

I recently talked with James Stewart; a military veteran turned pastor.

He said something profound: "Knowing you have superior weapons isn't enough in combat. "You must know how to use them and believe in them." The same applies to using the blood of Jesus in spiritual warfare.

Your Strategic Advantage

You must enlighten your understanding to see Jesus' complete defeat of Satan. Jesus Christ has dethroned him at the cross of Calvary and in His resurrection.

Therefore, you have a strategic advantage and move and fight from a position of victory.

As a believer, you have complete authority over any spiritual force.

You're more than a conqueror over all the enemy's power because of who you are in Christ (Luke 10:19; Rom. 8:37).

The Blood as Your Warfare Weapon

WHY IT'S SO POWERFUL

Victory Over Evil

The blood of Jesus gives you victory over Satan and evil forces. Revelation 12:11 declares, "They triumphed over him by the blood of the Lamb and by the word of their testimony."

You break all bondage and destroy strongholds by the blood of Jesus. You're assured of victory in any spiritual warfare.

Real-Life Victory: Maria's Breakthrough

"For years, I fought anxiety through willpower," Maria shares. "Then I learned to apply the blood of Jesus specifically in spiritual warfare. The difference was like night and day. What counselling couldn't fix, the blood overcame."

Practical Warfare Applications

DEFENSIVE WARFARE

Using the blood to:

- Create protective barriers.
- Shield your mind.
- Guard your family.
- Secure your territory.

Offensive Warfare

Applying the blood to:

- Break strongholds
- Advance God's kingdom
- Claim territory
- Defeat enemy plans

Battle Strategies Using the Blood

MORNING PREPARATION

1. Put on spiritual armour.
2. Apply the blood covering.
3. Declare your position.
4. Establish protection

During Spiritual Attack
Immediately:

1. Stand in blood authority.
2. Declare victory
3. Resist the enemy.
4. Maintain peace

Breaking Strongholds with the Blood
Identifying Strongholds
Look for:

- Persistent struggles
- Recurring patterns
- Stubborn resistance
- Generational issues

BREAKING PROCESS
Step by step:

1. Identify the stronghold
2. Declare blood authority
3. Command breakthrough

4. Stand in victory

Warfare Prayer Patterns

BASIC WARFARE PRAYER
"Through the blood of Jesus:

1. I take authority over this situation.
2. I break every stronghold.
3. I defeat every enemy.
4. I claim complete victory."

Advanced Battle Prayer
"By the power of the blood:

1. I destroy Satan's works.
2. I break all resistance.
3. I establish God's kingdom
4. I secure the total triumph."

Special Focus: Mind Battles

PROTECTING YOUR THOUGHTS
Apply the blood to:

- Thought patterns
- Mental strongholds
- Emotional struggles
- Decision processes

Victory Declarations
Speak forth:

1. "The blood protects my mind."

2. "No weapon formed against my thoughts shall prosper."
3. "The blood cleanses my mind."
4. "I have the mind of Christ."

Territorial Warfare

CLAIMING TERRITORY
Use the blood to:

- Cleanse atmospheres
- Claim spaces
- Establish authority
- Maintain victory

Strategic Application
For:

- Your home
- Workplace
- Ministry areas
- Communities

Warfare for Families

PROTECTING YOUR FAMILY
Cover:

- Each member
- Relationships
- Future generations
- Daily activities

Creating Family Shields
Establish:

- Blood barriers
- Covenant protection
- Spiritual guards
- Victory zones

Dealing with Specific Attacks

FINANCIAL WARFARE

Apply the blood to:

- Break poverty
- Release provision
- Establish abundance
- Maintain prosperity

Health Warfare

Use the blood for:

- Disease resistance
- Healing manifestation
- Strength renewal
- Complete wholeness

Relationship Warfare

Deploy the blood in:

- Conflict resolution
- Relationship healing
- Unity building
- Peace maintaining

Advanced Warfare Tactics

STRATEGIC TIMING
Know when to:

- Stand firm
- Advance
- Rest
- Press through

Warfare Wisdom
Understanding:

- Battle seasons
- Enemy tactics
- Victory timing
- Strategic rest

Emergency Battle Response

WHEN UNDER SUDDEN ATTACK

1. Immediately plead the blood
2. Stand in authority
3. Resist the enemy
4. Maintain position

Quick Victory Steps
Remember to:

- Stay calm
- Apply blood
- Declare victory
- Trust God

Training Others in Warfare

BASIC TRAINING
Teach:

- Blood authority
- Warfare principles
- Victory strategies
- Practical application

Advanced Mentoring
Guide in:

- Strategic warfare
- Territory claiming
- Stronghold breaking
- Victory maintaining

Your Warfare Action Plan

DAILY PREPARATION

1. Morning covering
2. Midday check
3. Evening securing
4. Continuous awareness

Weekly Strategy

1. Territory assessment
2. Victory review
3. Strategy adjustment
4. Team alignment

Warfare Declaration Guide

PERSONAL AUTHORITY

"In Jesus' name and through His blood:

1. I take authority over every attack.
2. I break every assignment of the enemy.
3. I destroy every work of darkness.
4. I establish victory in every area."

Team Warfare

"Together we declare:

1. Our territory is blood-covered.
2. Our victory is assured.
3. Our enemy is defeated.
4. Our triumph is complete."

A Warfare Prayer

"LORD JESUS, THANK YOU for Your victorious blood. I stand in its power today against every attack. Through Your blood, I claim complete victory. Help me fight effectively and maintain my triumphant position. In Your mighty name, Amen."

Looking Ahead

OUR NEXT CHAPTER WILL explore how to use the blood in healing ministry. Get ready to see how your warfare victory translates into healing power!

Remember: Every drop of Jesus's blood declares your victory in spiritual warfare. Stand confident in this truth!

"And they overcame him by the blood of the Lamb and by the word of their testimony, and they did not love their lives to the death."
- Revelation 12:11

Chapter 14: The Blood in Healing Ministry

I magine having the most powerful healing medicine in the universe. It could cure any disease, heal any wound, and restore any condition.

That's precisely what we have in the blood of Jesus.

Let's discover how to minister this healing power to others effectively.

Understanding Healing Ministry

PERSONAL STORY: THE ER Nurse's Revelation

Susanna, an ER nurse for 20 years, said, "In my training, we learned that blood carries life and healing."

"Realizing Jesus's blood has divine healing power changed my nursing and ministry."

The Blood's Healing Power

The blood of the Covenant gives complete healing and total restoration.

Pleading the blood and praying in Jesus' name in healing work brings perfect health.

Preparing for Healing Ministry

PERSONAL PREPARATION

When preparing for healing ministry, it's important to know your authority. You must be clear that you have blood-bought rights and divine backing.

1 Peter 2:24 declares, "He bore our sins in his body on the tree so that we might die to sins and live for righteousness; by his wounds, you have been healed."

Stay filled with the Holy Spirit and have compassion for the people you minister to.

In the 80s, he was on Pastor Reinhard Bonnke's healing ministry team. He would pray and fast to prepare for all his healing crusades.

Likewise, prepare yourself, walk healthy, and keep your channels clean.

Creating a Healing Atmosphere

PHYSICAL ENVIRONMENT

Set up:

- Peaceful space
- Comfortable seating
- Quiet atmosphere
- Minimal distractions

SPIRITUAL ENVIRONMENT

Establish:

- Faith atmosphere
- Expectant hearts
- Love presence
- Holy Spirit flow

Ministering Healing Through the Blood

BASIC HEALING STEPS

1. Interview Briefly
    - Listen carefully
    - Show compassion
    - Build faith
    - Create connection
2. Apply the Blood
    - Declare its power
    - Speak healing
    - Release faith
    - Expect results

Real-Life Miracle: John's Story

"Stage 4 cancer had spread throughout my body," John recalls. "When the healing team ministered to me using the blood of Jesus, something happened.

Scans three weeks later showed no trace of cancer. The doctors couldn't explain it, but we knew – it was the blood of Jesus."

Different Types of Healing Ministry

ONE-ON-ONE MINISTRY

Steps for individual ministry:

- Create connection
- Build faith
- Apply blood
- Release healing

Group Ministry

Strategies for crowds:

- Set atmosphere
- Build corporate faith
- Minister collectively
- Handle manifestations

Distance Ministry
Effective remote healing:

- Phone ministry
- Online sessions
- Prayer agreements
- Follow-up care

Specific Healing Applications

PHYSICAL HEALING
Apply the blood to:

- Disease conditions
- Chronic issues
- Injuries
- Pain

Emotional Healing
Minister to:

- Past trauma
- Deep wounds
- Mental health
- Relationship harm

Inner Healing

Address:

- Soul wounds
- Memory healing
- Identity restoration
- Heart wholeness

Power Declarations in Healing Ministry

PHYSICAL HEALING

"Through the blood of Jesus:

1. Disease must leave
2. Pain must go
3. Strength returns
4. Health manifests"

Emotional Healing

"By the power of the blood:

1. Trauma is healed
2. Peace is restored
3. Joy returns
4. Love flows"

Creating Faith for Healing

BUILDING FAITH THROUGH:

1. Scripture reading
2. Testimony sharing
3. Vision casting
4. Faith declaration

Maintaining Faith When:

- Symptoms persist
- Progress is slow
- Doubt arises
- Others question

Handling Special Cases

TERMINAL CONDITIONS

Minister with:

- Extra compassion
- Strong faith
- Wise words
- Patient love

Chronic Issues

Approach with:

- Understanding
- Persistence
- Hope
- Support

Following Up After Ministry

IMMEDIATE CARE

Provide:

- Clear instructions
- Faith reinforcement
- Prayer support
- Contact information

Long-term Support
Offer:

- Regular check-ins
- Continued prayer
- Faith building
- Victory celebration

Training Others in Healing Ministry

BASIC TRAINING
Teach:

- Blood foundation
- Simple steps
- Faith basics
- Practical application

Advanced Development
Guide in:

- Complex cases
- Team ministry
- Special situations
- Leadership skills

Your Healing Ministry Toolkit

ESSENTIAL TOOLS

1. Bible promises
2. Testimony collection
3. Declaration guide
4. Follow-up system

Supporting Resources

1. Teaching materials
2. Training videos
3. Ministry aids
4. Reference guides

Special Focus: Children's Healing Ministry

CHILD-FRIENDLY APPROACHES
Make it:

- Simple
- Fun
- Engaging
- Memorable

Parent Involvement
Include:

- Family training
- Home application
- Follow-up care
- Victory celebration

Creating a Healing Team

TEAM DEVELOPMENT
Build:

- Strong foundation
- Clear protocols
- United vision
- Effective ministry

Team Training
Provide:

- Regular teaching
- Practical experience
- Mentoring
- Growth opportunities

A Healing Minister's Prayer

"LORD JESUS, THANK YOU for Your healing blood. Help me minister Your healing power effectively. Let Your compassion flow through me. Use me as Your vessel of healing to touch lives. In Your name, Amen."

Looking Ahead

IN OUR NEXT CHAPTER, we'll explore how the blood brings deliverance from bondage. Get ready to discover freedom ministry!

Remember: Every drop of Jesus's blood carries healing power. Minister with confidence in this truth!

"By His stripes, we are healed." - Isaiah 53:5

Practical Ministry Guidelines

DO'S

1. Listen carefully
2. Show compassion
3. Build faith
4. Apply blood specifically

DON'TS

1. Rush the process
2. Promise specifics
3. Create dependency
4. Neglect follow-up

Your Ministry Action Plan

DAILY PREPARATION

1. Personal devotion
2. Faith building
3. Prayer covering
4. Compassion cultivation

Ministry Development

1. Continuous learning
2. Experience gathering
3. Team building
4. Effective service

There is power in the blood of Jesus in our redemption and healing.

Chapter 15: The Blood in Deliverance

Think of a master key that can unlock any prison door.

In deliverance ministry, the blood of Jesus frees all captives. It breaks every chain and opens every prison.

Let's discover how to use this powerful key effectively.

Understanding True Deliverance

PERSONAL STORY: THE Prison Chaplain's Insight

Pastor Mike, a 15-year prison chaplain, said, "I've seen people freed from prison but still bound inside."

I've seen others, still in jail, find freedom through Jesus' blood. "True deliverance happens from the inside out."

What Deliverance Is

It's more than emotional release, behaviour modification and religious ritual.

Deliverance gives complete freedom, identity restoration, and permanent change in one's life.

It includes deliverance from demons, but it covers a wider range. Our redemption is broader than just being freed from demons.

We are also delivered from sin, sickness, bad habits, and bondages.

The Blood's Role in Deliverance

WHY THE BLOOD WORKS

It works because it breaks legal rights, destroys strongholds, and removes bondages.

The blood establishes freedom and, through God's grace, delivers you.

Real-Life Freedom: Bongi's Story

"I struggled with addiction for 20 years," Bongi shares. "Rehab, therapy, willpower – nothing worked long-term. Everything changed when I finally learned to apply Jesus' blood in deliverance. I've been free for five years now."

Preparing for Deliverance Ministry

MINISTER PREPARATION

1. Personal Freedom
   - Walk in liberty
   - Maintain cleansing
   - Stay filled with Spirit
   - Keep authority clean
2. Spiritual Readiness
   - Know your authority
   - Build your faith
   - Sharpen discernment
   - Stay humble

The Deliverance Process

INITIAL ASSESSMENT
Look for:

- Root causes
- Entry points
- Legal rights
- Generational issues

Freedom Strategy
Develop:

- Specific approach
- Prayer Strategy
- Blood application
- Follow-up plan

Breaking Different Types of Bondage

PERSONAL BONDAGE
Such as:

- Addictions
- Fear patterns
- Destructive habits
- Wrong thinking

Generational Bondage
Including:

- Family curses
- Inherited patterns
- Bloodline issues
- Ancestral bonds

Spiritual Bondage
Addressing:

- Occult involvement
- False worship
- Soul ties
- Spiritual contracts

Practical Deliverance Steps

INTERVIEW PROCESS

- Listen carefully
- Ask wise questions
- Show compassion
- Build trust

Freedom Application

- Apply the blood
- Break bondages
- Cast out darkness
- Establish freedom

Freedom Maintenance

- Teach truth
- Build habits
- Provide support
- Monitor progress

Power Declarations in Deliverance

BREAKING BONDAGES

"Through the blood of Jesus:

1. Every chain is broken
2. All bondage ends
3. Freedom manifests
4. Liberty reigns"

Establishing Freedom

"By the power of the blood:

1. I am fully free
2. Old things are gone
3. New life flows
4. Victory remains"

Special Focus: Soul Ties

UNDERSTANDING SOUL Ties

Types:

- Relationship bonds
- Sexual connections
- Emotional attachments
- Spiritual agreements

Breaking Process

Steps:

1. Identify the tie
2. Renounce connection
3. Apply the blood
4. Declare freedom

Dealing with Stubborn Cases

WHEN FREEDOM SEEMS Delayed

Remember:

- Stay persistent
- Build faith
- Apply blood
- Trust process

Breakthrough Strategy
Implement:

1. Deeper investigation
2. Increased intensity
3. Team approach
4. Extended follow-up

Creating Freedom Environments

PHYSICAL SPACE
Set up:

- Private area
- Comfortable setting
- Minimal distractions
- Safe atmosphere

Spiritual Atmosphere
Establish:

- Faith environment
- Holy Spirit presence
- Peaceful atmosphere
- Victory expectation

Post-Deliverance Care

IMMEDIATE SUPPORT
Provide:

- Clear instructions
- Prayer coverage
- Contact information

- Emergency plan

Long-term Care
Offer:

- Regular check-ins
- Support group
- Growth Resources
- Victory coaching

Training Deliverance Teams

BASIC TRAINING
Teach:

- Biblical Foundation
- Blood authority
- Basic protocols
- Safety guidelines

Advanced Development
Guide in:

- Complex cases
- Team ministry
- Special situations
- Leadership skills

Freedom Maintenance Tools

DAILY PRACTICES
Encourage:

1. Blood application
2. Truth declaration
3. Worship lifestyle
4. Prayer discipline

Victory Habits
Develop:

1. Word meditation
2. Right relationships
3. Healthy boundaries
4. Spiritual growth

Handling Special Cases

YOUTH DELIVERANCE
Consider:

- Age appropriateness
- Parental involvement
- Simple approach
- Gentle process

Marriage Deliverance
Address:

- Both spouses
- Relationship issues
- Family patterns
- Future Freedom

A Deliverance Minister's Prayer

"LORD JESUS, THANK YOU for Your liberating blood. Use me as Your vessel of freedom. Help me minister deliverance effectively and compassionately. Let Your power flow through me to set captives free. In Your mighty name, Amen."

Emergency Deliverance Protocol

WHEN IMMEDIATE HELP Needed
Steps:

1. Quick assessment
2. Blood covering
3. Authority exercise
4. Freedom release

Follow-up Care
Provide:

1. Immediate support
2. Clear guidance
3. Prayer covering
4. Ongoing help

Your Deliverance Ministry Guide

ESSENTIAL TOOLS
Keep ready:

- Bible
- Declaration list
- Prayer guide
- Follow-up plan

Support Resources
Maintain:

- Team contacts
- Reference materials
- Care Network
- Emergency numbers

Looking Ahead

IN PART 5, WE'LL EXPLORE the future implications of the blood's power. Get ready to see how this truth impacts eternity!

Remember: Every drop of Jesus's blood declares "FREEDOM!" over bound lives. Minister with confidence in this truth!

"Therefore if the Son makes you free, you shall be free indeed." - John 8:36

Chapter 16: End-Time Victory Through the Blood

Have you ever noticed how the final chapter of a great story brings everything together?

As history's grand finale nears, the blood of Jesus takes centre stage.

Let's discover how this powerful truth ensures your victory in the days ahead.

Understanding End-Time Power

PERSONAL STORY: THE Veteran's Vision

Recently, I spoke with Pastor James, who's been in ministry for over 50 years. He shared something profound: "In all my years of ministry, I've never seen the blood of Jesus more relevant than now." It's as if God saved the most significant demonstrations of its power for these final chapters of history."

Why the Blood Matters More Now

Because it:

- Overcomes increasing darkness.
- Provides supernatural protection.
- Ensures final victory.
- Secures eternal triumph.

Prophecies About the Blood's Power

BIBLICAL PREDICTIONS

Looking at:

- Revelation insights
- Prophet's words
- Apostolic warnings
- Jesus's promises

End-Time Perspective: Daniel's Vision
"And they overcame by the blood of the Lamb" refers to believers in the final days. It takes on new meaning when we understand this.

The Blood in Tribulation Times

PROTECTION PROVISION
The blood provides:

- Divine Covering
- Supernatural shelter
- Miraculous provision
- Complete security

Victory Assurance
Guaranteeing:

- Overcoming power
- Unshakeable faith
- Enduring strength
- Final triumph

Preparing for Future Challenges

PERSONAL PREPARATION
Develop:

1. Deep blood understanding
2. Strong faith foundation
3. Warfare experience
4. Victory mindset

Family Preparation
Establish:

1. Blood covenant awareness
2. Family faith practices
3. Victory traditions
4. Generational impact

The Blood and End-Time Events

DURING GROWING DARKNESS
The blood:

- Illuminates' truth
- Guides paths
- Protects minds
- Strengthens hearts

IN TIMES OF PERSECUTION
Providing:

- Supernatural courage
- Divine wisdom
- Heavenly protection
- Overcoming power

Special Focus: The Rapture Connection

THE BLOOD'S ROLE

Understanding:

- Redemption completion
- Body transformation
- Heaven's preparation
- Glory revelation

Your Preparation

Steps for:

- Ready position
- Pure heart
- Active faith
- Expectant spirit

End-Time Declaration Guide

VICTORY DECLARATIONS

"Through the blood of Jesus:

1. I overcome every challenge.
2. I stand unshakable.
3. I triumph in trials.
4. I finish strong."

Protection Declarations

"By the power of the blood:

1. I am divinely protected.
2. My family is secure.
3. My faith stands strong.

4. My victory is assured"

Creating End-Time Victory Habits

DAILY PRACTICES
Establish:

1. Blood application
2. Faith declaration
3. Victory mindset
4. Overcoming lifestyle

Weekly Rhythms
Include:

1. Deep study
2. Family Preparation
3. Corporate strength
4. Victory celebration

The Blood and Global Events

WORLD SITUATIONS
Applying blood power to:

- Economic challenges
- Social upheaval
- Natural disasters
- Spiritual warfare

Kingdom Advance
Seeing:

- Gospel acceleration

- Power demonstrations
- Mass salvation
- Supernatural signs

Preparing Others for End Times

TEACHING POINTS
Share about:

1. Blood's relevance
2. Victory assurance
3. Preparation needs
4. Overcoming power

Training Focus
Develop:

1. Strong foundation
2. Practical application
3. Victory mindset
4. Enduring faith

The Blood's Final Triumph

ULTIMATE VICTORY
Witnessing:

- Satan's defeat
- Evil's destruction
- Truth's vindication
- Christ's exaltation

Eternal Impact
Celebrating:

- Complete redemption
- Perfect restoration
- Eternal glory
- Endless victory

Special Challenges and Solutions

ECONOMIC PRESSURES
Apply blood for:

- Supernatural provision
- Divine protection
- Miracle supply
- Abundant resources

Social Persecution
Stand in:

- Blood authority
- Unshakeable faith
- Divine courage
- Overcoming power

Your End-Time Action Plan

PERSONAL STEPS

1. Deepen blood understanding
2. Strengthen faith foundation
3. Build victory habits
4. Maintain readiness

Family Preparation

1. Teach blood truths
2. Establish practices
3. Create traditions
4. Build strength together

Victory Testimonies for Future Faith

MARCIA'S PROVISION Story

"During severe economic collapse, we saw the blood's power provide supernaturally. What seemed impossible became our daily reality."

The Chen Family's Protection

"During persecution, the blood of Jesus shielded our family." We experienced protection that defied natural explanation."

End-Time Prayer Guide

DAILY COVER

"Lord Jesus, through Your blood:

1. Cover my day completely.
2. Protect my family entirely.
3. Guide my steps perfectly.
4. Secure my victory.

Crisis Response

"In Your name and through Your blood:

1. I stand unshakable.
2. I walk in victory.
3. I overcome challenges.

4. I finish strong.

A Prayer for End-Time Victory

"PRECIOUS LORD JESUS, thank You for Your powerful blood that ensures my victory these last days. Help me stand strong, overcome every challenge, and finish my race with triumph. Let Your blood's power be fully demonstrated in and through my life. In Your mighty name, Amen."

Looking Ahead

IN OUR FINAL CHAPTER, we'll explore the eternal benefits of the blood. Get ready to see how this power extends into eternity!

Remember: Every drop of Jesus's blood guarantees your victory in these last days. Stand confidently in this truth!

"And they overcame him by the blood of the Lamb and by the word of their testimony, and they did not love their lives to the death." - Revelation 12:11

Chapter 17: Eternal Benefits of the Blood

Have you ever received an inheritance that changed your life? The blood of Jesus gives an eternal inheritance. It transforms your life on earth and lasts forever.

Let's explore the fantastic benefits that never end.

Understanding Your Eternal Inheritance

PERSONAL STORY: THE Diamond Ring

My grandmother once showed me a family diamond. "It's precious," she said. "It's been in our family for generations, but it will wear out."

Then she smiled and added, "But the benefits of Jesus's blood? They're forever." That simple contrast showed me our eternal, blood-bought inheritance.

More Than Just Getting to Heaven

It includes:

- Eternal relationship
- Endless privileges
- Everlasting benefits
- Forever fellowship

Heavenly Rewards Through the Blood

IMMEDIATE HEAVEN BENEFITS

1. Perfect Welcome

- ° Complete acceptance
- ° Full belonging
- ° Instant recognition
- ° Total welcome
2. Family Status
    - ° Royal position
    - ° Divine privileges
    - ° Eternal standing
    - ° Heavenly rights

REAL-LIFE GLIMPSE: Pastor Tom's Near-Death Experience

"After being clinically dead for four minutes," Pastor Tom shares, "I felt the power of the blood in heaven." "With the acceptance complete, the welcome was overwhelming. I now understood, in a new way, why the blood was so precious."

The Eternal Power of the Blood

NEVER-ENDING BENEFITS

The blood eternally:

- Speaks for you
- Represents you
- Qualifies you
- Empowers you

Lasting Impact

Forever providing:

- Access to God
- Divine fellowship

- Kingdom Authority
- Heavenly privileges

Your Eternal Identity

WHO YOU ARE FOREVER

- Blood-bought child
- Royal heir
- Eternal family member
- Heaven's citizen

What You Have Forever

- Complete acceptance
- Full privileges
- Total access
- Perfect standing

The Blood in Heaven's Economy

ETERNAL CURRENCY

Understanding how:

- It never devalues
- Always speaks
- Forever works
- Eternally qualifies

Heavenly Resources

Accessing:

- Unlimited provision
- Eternal riches
- Divine resources
- Heavenly wealth

Special Focus: Eternal Fellowship

WITH GOD

Enjoying:

- Perfect communion
- Complete intimacy
- Endless fellowship
- Total acceptance

With Family

Experiencing:

- Restored relationships
- Perfect unity
- Eternal bonds
- Complete harmony

The Blood's Eternal Voice

WHAT IT DECLARES FOREVER

Speaking:

1. Your Acceptance
2. Your position
3. Your rights
4. Your privileges

Its Ongoing Work

Continuing to:

1. Represent you
2. Qualify you
3. Empower you
4. Advocate for you

Preparing for Eternal Benefits

PRESENT PREPARATIONS

Start now:

1. Understanding your rights
2. Walking in privileges
3. Living from position
4. Enjoying benefits

Future Anticipation

Looking forward to:

1. Full manifestation
2. Complete realization
3. Perfect experience
4. Eternal enjoyment

Eternal Victory Celebration

THE NEVER-ENDING TRIUMPH

Celebrating:

- Complete victory
- Perfect freedom
- Eternal joy
- Endless peace

The Eternal Song
Joining in:

- Blood praise
- Victory Worship
- Eternal thanksgiving
- Forever adoration

Teaching About Eternal Benefits

KEY POINTS TO SHARE
Help others understand:

1. Present reality
2. Future fullness
3. Eternal nature
4. Forever benefits

Practical Application
Guide in:

1. Present walking
2. Future preparing
3. Eternal thinking
4. Forever living

Your Eternal Perspective Guide

DAILY LIVING
View life through:

- Eternal lens
- Blood benefits
- Forever perspective

- Kingdom vision

Future Focus
Keep sight of:

- Coming Glory
- Perfect fulfilment
- Complete manifestation
- Eternal reality

Eternal Declarations

SPEAK THESE TRUTHS:

1. "I am eternally accepted through the blood."
2. "Heaven's resources are mine forever."
3. "My blood-bought rights are eternal."
4. "I have everlasting fellowship with God."

A Prayer of Eternal Perspective

"HEAVENLY FATHER, THANK You for the eternal benefits of Jesus's blood. Help me live today in light of forever. Let me enjoy my hard-won rights now while I await their full use in eternity. In Jesus's name, Amen."

Special Applications

IN DAILY CHALLENGES
Remember:

- Temporary nature
- Eternal perspective
- Blood benefits
- Forever victory

In Life Decisions
Consider:

- Eternal impact
- Forever value
- Kingdom perspective
- Blood benefits

Your Eternal Benefits Checklist

PRESENT ENJOYMENT
Access now:

1. Divine fellowship
2. Kingdom Authority
3. Heavenly resources
4. Blood benefits

Future Anticipation
Look forward to:

1. Perfect manifestation
2. Complete experience
3. Eternal fullness
4. Forever joy

Final Thoughts on the Blood

ITS ETERNAL NATURE
Remember:

- Never loses power
- Always effective
- Forever Active

- Eternally speaking

Its Lasting Impact
Celebrating:

- Eternal redemption
- Forever acceptance
- Endless love
- Everlasting life

Looking Back and Forward

WHAT WE'VE LEARNED
Reflecting on:

- Blood's power
- Present benefits
- Future victory
- Eternal impact

Where We're Going
Anticipating:

- Perfect fulfilment
- Complete manifestation
- Eternal enjoyment
- Forever celebration

Closing Prayer

"THANK YOU, LORD JESUS, for your eternal word that will always endure. *As I close this study, help me live fully aware of its eternal benefits. Let every day be lived in light of my blood-bought forever inheritance. In Your name, Amen.*"

Remember: Every drop of Jesus's blood secured eternal, unending benefits. They will never diminish. Live today in light of forever!

"And they sang a new song, saying: 'You are worthy... for You were slain, and have redeemed us to God by Your blood.'" - Revelation 5:9

Conclusion: Living in Blood-Bought Victory

As we end our journey, let's reflect.

We've discovered an incredible truth. The blood of Jesus isn't just a historical fact or a religious idea. It's a living, powerful reality that transforms our lives.

Our Journey Together

PERSONAL REFLECTION

When we began this study of the blood's power, you might have been like many others. You knew it was necessary but needed to figure out why or how.

Now, I hope you see it differently. Like Sarah, who said, "I used to sing about the blood in church without really understanding." Now, I can't go a day without applying its power in my life!"

What We've Discovered

Together, we've learned:

- The historical foundation of the blood covenant
- The perfect sacrifice of Jesus
- The seven-fold power of His blood
- Practical applications for daily life
- Special ministry applications
- Future and eternal implications

Making It Your Own

PERSONAL APPLICATION

Remember:

1. Every truth we've covered is personally yours
2. Each promise is available now
3. All power is accessible today
4. Every benefit belongs to you

Daily Living

Start implementing:

1. Morning blood covering
2. Daily declarations
3. Practical applications
4. Victory living

Key Principles to Remember

THE BLOOD IS:

1. Always Available
   - 24/7 access
   - Constant power
   - Continuous effectiveness
   - Present help
2. Always Effective
   - Never fails
   - Always works
   - Perfectly sufficient
   - Completely reliable

Your Next Steps

IMMEDIATE ACTIONS
Begin with:

1. Daily blood application
2. Regular declarations
3. Practical steps
4. Faith actions

Long-term Growth
Develop:

1. Deeper understanding
2. Stronger faith
3. Consistent practice
4. Teaching others

Creating Your Victory Lifestyle

DAILY HABITS
Establish:

- Morning dedication
- Midday reinforcement
- Evening review
- Continuous awareness

Weekly Patterns
Include:

- Deeper study
- Family application
- Corporate Worship

- Victory celebration

Overcoming Common Challenges

WHEN DOUBT COMES
Remember:

- The blood never fails
- Your position is secure
- Victory is guaranteed
- Power is available

When Results Seem Delayed
Stand firm:

- Keep declaring
- Maintain faith
- Stay consistent
- Trust the process

Teaching Others

SIMPLE STEPS TO SHARE
Help others:

1. Understand basics
2. Start simple practices
3. Build faith
4. See results

Growing Together
Create:

- Study groups

- Prayer partnerships
- Support networks
- Victory celebrations

Your Victory Declaration Guide

DAILY DECLARATIONS
Speak forth:

1. "I am blood-bought and victory-bound."
2. "The blood never loses its power in my life."
3. "I walk in blood-bought authority today."
4. "Victory is my constant reality."

Situation-Specific Declarations
Apply to:

- Health challenges
- Financial needs
- Relationship issues
- Ministry opportunities

Moving Forward in Victory

REMEMBER THESE TRUTHS

1. The blood always works
2. Victory is your inheritance
3. Power is available now
4. Results are guaranteed

Walk in These Realities

1. Confident faith

2. Consistent application
3. Continuous growth
4. Contagious victory

A Final Prayer Together

"PRECIOUS LORD JESUS, Thank You for this journey of discovering the power of Your blood. As we move forward, help us live daily in the full reality of what Your blood has purchased. Let our lives be living testimonies of its power. Please help us share this truth with others and walk in increasing victory.

Thank you for noting that this isn't the end but the beginning. It's a lifetime of discovering and applying the power of Your blood. We choose to live in blood-bought victory today and every day.

In Your mighty name, Amen."

Your Victory Commitment

I encourage you to make this personal commitment:

"I choose to live in the full power of the blood of Jesus. I will:

- Apply its truth daily
- Share its power regularly
- Walk in its victory consistently
- Celebrate its benefits continually"

Final Encouragement

REMEMBER: EVERY CHALLENGE you face has already been overcome by the blood of Jesus. Every victory you need has already been purchased. Every blessing you require has already been provided.

Live today and every day in the conscious awareness that you are:

- Blood-bought
- Victory-assured

- Power-filled
- Destiny-bound

The journey we've shared in these pages isn't ending—it's just beginning. Go forth and live in the full power of Jesus's blood!

"Now may the God of peace who brought up our Lord Jesus from the dead, that great Shepherd of the sheep, through the blood of the everlasting covenant, make you complete in every good work to do His will, working in you what is well pleasing in His sight, through Jesus Christ, to whom be glory forever and ever. Amen." - Hebrews 13:20-21

Appendices

Appendix A: Scripture References for Victory Living

The Foundation of Blood Power

1. Life-Giving Blood Scriptures
    - Leviticus 17:11 - "For the life of the flesh is in the blood."
    - Hebrews 9:22 - "Without shedding blood, there is no remission."
    - 1 John 1:7 - "The blood of Jesus cleanses us from all sin."
    - Revelation 12:11 - "They overcame by the blood of the Lamb."

2. Protection Through the Blood
    - Exodus 12:13 - The Passover protection
    - Hebrews 13:20-21 - The everlasting covenant
    - Revelation 7:14 - Washed white in the blood
    - Psalm 91:1-16 - Divine protection promises

3. Healing in the Blood
    - Isaiah 53:5 - "By His stripes, we are healed"
    - 1 Peter 2:24 - Healing through His wounds
    - Mark 5:25-34 - The woman with the issue of blood
    - James 5:14-16 - Prayer of faith for healing

Victory Declarations from Scripture

1. Overcoming Scriptures
    - Romans 8:37 - More than conquerors
    - 2 Corinthians 2:14 - Always leads in triumph
    - 1 John 5:4 - Faith overcomes the world
    - Philippians 4:13 - Strength through Christ
2. Authority Scriptures
    - Luke 10:19 - Authority over all enemy power
    - Mark 16:17-18 - Signs following believers
    - Ephesians 2:6 - Seated in heavenly places
    - 2 Corinthians 10:4-5 - Mighty weapons

Appendix B: Power-Filled Prayers and Declarations

MORNING VICTORY PRAYERS

Daily Blood Coverage Prayer

"Father, in Jesus' name, I apply the blood of Jesus over:

- My spirit, soul, and body
- My mind, will, and emotions.
- My family and loved ones
- My home and possessions
- My work and ministry."

Protection Declaration

"Through the precious blood of Jesus:

1. I am protected from all harm.
2. No weapon formed against me prospers.
3. Evil must pass over my life.
4. Angels guard my way today."

Warfare Prayers
Standing in Victory
"By the power of Jesus' blood:

1. Every stronghold is broken.
2. Every chain falls off.
3. Every obstacle moves
4. Every enemy flees."

Breakthrough Prayer
"Through the blood of Jesus:

1. Doors of blessing open
2. Resources are released
3. Victory manifests
4. Abundance flows"

Appendix C: Study and Discussion Guide

PERSONAL STUDY QUESTIONS

For each chapter:

1. Key Revelations
   ◦ What new truth did you discover?
   ◦ How does this change your understanding?
   ◦ Where can you apply this truth?
2. Personal Application
   ◦ What needs to change in your life?
   ◦ How will you implement this truth?
   ◦ When will you start applying it?
3. Victory Steps

- List three actions you'll take
- Identify potential challenges
- Plan your strategy for victory.

Group Discussion Guide
Session Format

1. Opening (15 minutes)
    - Worship
    - Testimony sharing
    - Prayer
2. Discussion (30 minutes)
    - Chapter review
    - Key points emphasis
    - Personal applications
3. Application (15 minutes)
    - Group prayer
    - Declaration time
    - Victory celebration

Growth Journal Prompts
Daily Reflection

1. Today's Victory
    - What breakthroughs did you see?
    - How did you apply the blood?
    - What victories can you celebrate?
2. Learning Points
    - New insights gained
    - Truths reinforced
    - Areas for growth
3. Tomorrow's Focus
    - Faith goals

- ∘ Victory plans
- ∘ Prayer points

Appendix D: Victory Testimonies

HEALING TESTIMONIES

1. Physical Healing "After applying the blood daily over my cancer diagnosis, doctors were amazed to find no trace of the disease three months later." - Sarah M.
2. Emotional Healing "Years of trauma healed as I learned to apply the blood to my emotional wounds." - James R.
3. Financial Breakthrough "Understanding blood covenant provision transformed our financial situation completely." - The Johnson Family.

Deliverance Stories

1. Freedom from Addiction "Twenty years of addiction broken through understanding the power of the blood." - Michael T.
2. Family Restoration "Our marriage was restored as we learned to apply blood covenant principles." - The Andersons
3. Business Transformation "Our company went from bankruptcy to prosperity through blood covenant principles." - Robert K.

Protection Testimonies

1. Divine Safety "Our home was untouched while others around us were destroyed in the storm." - The Williams Family.
2. Supernatural Provision "Resources appeared exactly when needed, proving God's covenant faithfulness." - Pastor Tom.
3. Ministry Impact "Applying these principles in ministry has led

to countless miracles." - Evangelist Mary.

Quick Reference Tools

EMERGENCY RESPONSE Guide

When facing sudden challenges:

1. Immediately plead the blood.
2. Stand in faith
3. Declare victory
4. Maintain peace
5. Expect results

Daily Victory Checklist

✓ Morning blood application ✓ Victory declarations ✓ Faith actions ✓ Gratitude expressions ✓ Evening review

Victory Declaration Cards

(PRINT THESE CARDS, carry them with you, and declare them daily)

Protection Declaration Cards

CARD 1: PERSONAL PROTECTION

FRONT: "Through the Blood of Jesus, I Am Protected"

- "No weapon formed against me shall prosper" (Isaiah 54:17)
- "A thousand may fall at my side, but it shall not come near me" (Psalm 91:7)

BACK: Daily Declaration: "I declare through the blood of Jesus:

1. I am surrounded by divine protection

2. Every attack must pass over me
3. Angels guard my path today
4. No harm can touch me."

Card 2: Family Protection
FRONT: "My Family Is Blood-Covered"

- "As for me and my house, we will serve the Lord" (Joshua 24:15)
- "The blood shall be a sign...and no plague shall destroy you" (Exodus 12:13)

BACK: Family Shield Declaration: "Through the blood of Jesus:

1. My family walks in divine safety
2. Our home is protected
3. Our relationships are guarded
4. Our future is secure."

Healing Declaration Cards

CARD 3: PHYSICAL HEALING
FRONT: "By His Stripes I Am Healed"

- "By His stripes, we are healed" (Isaiah 53:5)
- "I am the Lord who heals you" (Exodus 15:26)

BACK: Healing Power Declaration: "Through the blood of Jesus:

1. My body is healed
2. Disease must leave
3. Pain must go
4. Strength flows in me."

Card 4: Emotional Healing
FRONT: "Emotional Wholeness Through the Blood"

- "He heals the brokenhearted" (Psalm 147:3)
- "The joy of the Lord is my strength" (Nehemiah 8:10)

BACK: Emotional Freedom Declaration: "By the power of the blood:

1. My heart is healed
2. Peace fills my mind
3. Joy overflows
4. Love restores me."

Provision Declaration Cards

CARD 5: FINANCIAL PROVISION
FRONT: "Blood Covenant Provision Is Mine"

- "My God shall supply all your need" (Philippians 4:19)
- "The blessing of the Lord makes rich" (Proverbs 10:22)

BACK: Provision Declaration: "Through the blood covenant:

1. All my needs are met
2. Resources flow to me
3. Abundance surrounds me
4. Prosperity is mine."

Card 6: Business Victory
FRONT: "Business Success Through the Blood"

- "Whatever he does shall prosper" (Psalm 1:3)
- "You shall be blessed in all your undertakings" (Deuteronomy

28:6)

BACK: Business Breakthrough Declaration: "By covenant power:

1. My business prospers
2. Clients are attracted
3. Resources multiply
4. Success manifests"

Victory Declaration Cards

CARD 7: SPIRITUAL VICTORY
FRONT: "Overcoming Through the Blood"

- "We are more than conquerors" (Romans 8:37)
- "They overcame by the blood of the Lamb" (Revelation 12:11)

BACK: Victory Declaration: "Through the blood of Jesus:

1. I am an overcomer
2. Victory is mine
3. Success follows me
4. Triumph is certain."

Card 8: Authority Declaration
FRONT: "Blood-Bought Authority"

- "All authority has been given to Me" (Matthew 28:18)
- "Behold, I give you authority" (Luke 10:19)

BACK: Authority Declaration: "In Jesus' name and by His blood:

1. I walk into the authority
2. Demons must flee

3. Circumstances change
4. Mountains move"

Emergency Response Cards

CARD 9: CRISIS VICTORY
FRONT: "Immediate Victory Through the Blood"

- "God is our refuge and strength" (Psalm 46:1)
- "The Lord shall fight for you" (Exodus 14:14)

BACK: Emergency Declaration: "Right now, through the blood:

1. Peace comes
2. Victory manifests
3. Help arrives
4. Solutions appear"

Card 10: Warfare Victory
FRONT: "Instant Breakthrough Power"

- "The battle is the Lord's" (1 Samuel 17:47)
- "Thanks be to God who gives us the victory" (1 Corinthians 15:57)

BACK: Warfare Declaration: "By the blood of Jesus:

1. Every attack is defeated
2. Every weapon fails
3. Every obstacle moves
4. Every victory comes."

How to Use These Cards

DAILY USE

1. Morning Preparation
     - Select appropriate cards
     - Declare with faith
     - Carry key cards with you
     - Review throughout day
2. Specific Situations
     - Choose relevant card
     - Declare with authority
     - Stand in faith
     - Expect results

Card Organization

- Print on sturdy card stock
- Consider laminating
- Keep in convenient groups
- Carry card holder

Declaration Tips

1. Speak with authority
2. Declare in faith
3. Maintain consistency
4. Expect manifestation

Teaching Others

- Share card copies
- Explain declaration power
- Demonstrate proper use
- Encourage daily practice

Remember: These cards are your portable power tools. They're not magical formulas. They're faith declarations in Jesus's blood. Use them consistently and expectantly!

Note: You may customize these declarations. But keep their biblical and blood covenant basis.

Remember: These resources are your practical tools for living in blood-bought victory. Use them daily, share them freely, and celebrate the results!

9 798230 292623